The Philosophy of Childhood

The
Philosophy
of Childhood

―――

Gareth B. Matthews

HARVARD UNIVERSITY PRESS
Cambridge, Massachusetts
London, England
1994

This book is printed on acid-free paper, and its binding materials
have been chosen for strength and durability.

Library of Congress Cataloging-in-Publication Data
Matthews, Gareth B., 1929–
The philosophy of childhood / Gareth B. Matthews.
p.   cm.
Includes bibliographical references and index.
ISBN 0-674-66480-9 (acid-free paper)
1. Children and philosophy.   2. Child psychology—Philosophy.   I. Title.
B105.C45M38   1994
108'.3—dc20
94-16178
CIP

For Sarah, Becca, and John

Contents

Introduction: Getting the Idea

*I*t was 1963 when I first connected philosophy with childhood. Our family cat, Fluffy, had contracted fleas. I announced that I would have to take Fluffy into the basement to fumigate her. Our older daughter, Sarah, then four years old, asked if she could watch. Reluctantly I agreed—with the proviso that Sarah should stand high on the stairs, so that she would not herself breathe in the anti-flea dust I was about to administer to the cat.

From her perch at the head of the stairs, Sarah watched this primitive ritual with great interest. "Daddy," she asked after a while, "how did Fluffy get fleas?"

"Oh," I replied nonchalantly, "she must have been playing with another cat; fleas must have jumped off the other cat onto Fluffy."

Sarah reflected. "How did *that* cat get fleas?" she asked.

"Oh, it must have been playing with yet another cat," I answered jauntily; "they must have jumped off that cat onto the one Fluffy later played with."

Sarah paused. "But Daddy," she said earnestly, "it can't go on and on like that forever; the only thing that goes on and on like that forever is numbers!"

At the time of this incident I was teaching philosophy at the University of Minnesota. One of the standard topics in several of the courses I taught there was the Cosmological Argument for the existence of God. That argument depends upon ruling out an infinite regress of causes, so as to prove the existence of the First Cause, which, St. Thomas Aquinas assures us with surprising aplomb, we all call "God." I can remember thinking, "Here I am teaching my university students the argument for a First Cause, and my four-year-old daughter comes up, on her own, with an argument for the First Flea!"

At that time I knew very little about developmental psychology. Oh, I knew something about Jean Piaget. I had even heard him lecture (in French! which was a challenge for me) when I was a graduate student in philosophy at Harvard. I certainly knew something about Piaget's famous conservation experiments. But I did not understand that Piaget's theory made no allowance whatsoever for the philosophical thinking of my daughter, who, according to Piagetian theory, still lingered in the antechamber of "pre-operational thought."

I can remember telling the story of Sarah and the fleas from time to time, at parties, usually. But I had no inkling that I might one day try to make a case for the naturalness with which, like Sarah, many young children do philosophy on their own initiative. Certainly I did not appreciate the many connections between philosophy and childhood that I hope to bring out in this book.

Some six years after the flea incident, my family and I moved east, where I took up a position at the University of Massachusetts. Our arrival in Massachusetts coincided with the local onset of what was then called, rather patronizingly, I thought, "student unrest." At my new campus there were strikes, bomb scares, and countless demonstrations. I was myself quite opposed to the Vietnam war. So, although already ten years away from being a student, I joined in at least some of this "student unrest." More than once I went with busloads of protesters, mostly students, to Washington to register my own dissent.

At this time I noticed a phenomenon in my philosophy classroom that slowly began to trouble me. Some of my best students—certainly not all of them, but some of the most appealing ones—expressed to me the suspicion that philosophy was a plot by "the Establishment" to distract the attention of college students, especially male students, from the issues of life and death raised by the Vietnam war.

How could anyone possibly think that my beloved philosophy was an Establishment plot? I was hurt. I didn't know how to respond. How does one deal with a suspicion like that?

Thanks especially to the pioneering work of Matthew Lipman and his associates at the Institute for the Advancement of Philosophy for Children in Montclair, New Jersey, philosophy is today gradually making its appearance throughout the school curriculum, kindergarten through twelfth grade. But two decades ago, at the time of this Vietnam "unrest," philosophy was almost the only prominent college subject that a student would probably not have encountered in any curricular form before college. Anyone even slightly paranoid about "the Establishment" might well find this striking fact suspicious.

As I, in fact, believed, some parts of philosophy might actually help a student think more deeply and more clearly about the issues of war and peace. But most parts would not do that, or at least not do so directly. I did not want to hold my discussions of, say, Descartes's "I think, therefore I am," or Aquinas's Cosmological Argument, hostage to some dubious connection between them and issues in, say, Just War Theory, or questions about the limits of morality.

One night, while I was reading a bedtime story to my son, John, then about three years old, it occurred to me that the story I was reading raised a philosophical issue that I planned to discuss with my university students the next day. So I took the story along to class on the following day. I began my lecture by reading the story I had brought from home. (I can no longer remember for sure what the story was, but it may have been James Thurber's *Many Moons*, a favorite of all my children. That story deals whimsically with perceptual illusions, and especially with the apparent size of the moon.) "Can you remember thinking about this problem when you were little?" I asked my students after I had read them the story. "If you can," I continued, "the class today will give you a chance to return to familiar territory."

My aim was—and is, for I sometimes follow this practice even today—to convince my students that philosophy is a natural activity, quite as natural as making music and playing games. To be sure, the study of philosophy has certain practical uses. It is good preparation for certain vocations, like the law, that reward clear thinking and strong reasoning. But, like poetry, philosophy is also its own reward.

I'm not sure how successful I was in winning over my Vietnam-era cynics. But I certainly did sharpen my own realization of the fact that there is an important strand of children's literature that is genuinely philosophical. I am fond of telling anyone who will listen that, for example, Arnold Lobel's *Frog and Toad Together*, which is so simple in its vocabulary as to count as an "I can read book," is also a philosophical classic (see Chapter 9).

It was a natural next step in my slow awakening to the connections between philosophy and children to write a paper on philosophy and children's literature. At the urging of a friend I submitted the paper to the program committee of the American Philosophical Association, Pacific Division, and, when it was accepted, read it to a gathering of philosophers in San Francisco. I found, somewhat to my surprise, that not just elementary school teachers but even other professional philosophers were interested in the connections I could demonstrate between philosophy and children's literature. I then became interested in exploring the philosophical thinking in children to which the authors of philosophical children's stories were appealing. That brought me back to Sarah and the fleas.

Eventually I wrote *Philosophy and the Young Child* (Harvard, 1980), which has as its main thesis that some children naturally raise questions, make comments, and even engage in reasoning that professional philosophers can recognize as philosophical. When, at the very beginning of that book, Tim, age six, asks, "Papa, how can we be sure that everything is not a dream?" he raises one of the oldest and most persistently baffling questions in philosophy. And when Tim later seeks to reassure his father with the reasoning, "If it was a dream, we wouldn't go around asking if it was a dream," he offers a solution to this problem that can be usefully compared with the responses of Plato and Descartes.

My informal research suggests that such spontaneous excursions into philosophy are not at all unusual for children between the ages of three and seven; in somewhat older children, though, even eight- and nine-year-olds, they become rare, or at least rarely reported. My hypothesis is that, once children become well settled into school, they learn that only "useful" questioning is expected of them. Philosophy then either goes underground, to be pursued privately, perhaps, and not shared with others, or else becomes totally dormant.

To establish for myself that somewhat older children can, if deliberately provoked, still respond imaginatively and resourcefully to philosophical questions, I developed the technique of writing story-beginnings in which the characters, mostly children, stumble, unaided by adults, on some philosophical issue or problem. Freddie, say, goes aboard an old ship, which, he learns, has had 85 percent of her boards replaced. During the shipboard tour Freddie feels proud to be able to walk the decks of "the oldest square-rigger afloat." But his older sister, when she hears of the piece-by-piece replacement of most of the original boards, ridicules Freddie's boast. "With 85 percent of the boards brand new, that ship could hardly be an old one, never mind the oldest square-rigger afloat," she sneers. At this expression of skepticism my story-beginning comes to an end.

With a story-beginning like this in hand I visited classrooms, where I asked the children how the story ought to go on. Without hesitation they launched into spirited discussions of the vexing questions of identity through time that the story raises. They compared ships to bicycles or cars, whose original parts are gradually replaced over time. They sometimes even discussed the gradual displacement of cells in their own bodies. And they soon took up recognizable positions on the requirements for a ship, or a bicycle, or a human body to persist through time.

One child might say that there is a new ship when more than half the timbers have been replaced. Another might allow that the old ship still sails the seas as long as at least one(!) of the original boards remains. Still another might suggest that there is a new ship as soon as the very first board is replaced. Someone would single out one particular part of the vessel as essential for the persistence of the old ship—the keel, perhaps, or the mast, or the wheel. Someone else might be satisfied that the old ship still sails the seas as long as the replacement of boards is gradual and the ship continues to sail her familiar routes.

I have used this story-beginning technique in various schools in this country and abroad. My book *Dialogues with Children* (Harvard, 1984) is an account of my successes with it in a small class of eight-to-eleven-year-olds in a music school in Scotland. The book is also an introduction to philosophy through the voices (and minds!) of children.

So far I have talked about children as philosophers. How might one get from that topic to the idea that there could be such a subject as the philosophy of childhood?

My own journey began with reflections on why it seems surprising that young children, many of them, are naturally philosophical. What ideas about children and the nature of childhood had I previously accepted, I asked myself, that made it so surprising to me that children would naturally take to philosophy? Perhaps the very notion of a child was elusive or problematic in a way that I had not appreciated, had not even stopped to consider.

Four years before the publication of my *Dialogues with Children,*

Matthew Lipman had in fact suggested in a symposium at the annual meetings of the American Philosophical Association that we might think of the philosophy of childhood in analogy to the philosophy of religion, the philosophy of science, the philosophy of art, the philosophy of history, and the many other, already familiar, "philosophy of *x*" subjects currently recognized in college curricula.

Just as people say all sorts of philosophically problematic things about God, about quantum physics, about what counts as a work of art, or the cause of some historical event, so they also say philosophically problematic things about childhood. So Mat's suggestion was, in effect, that we philosophers might well turn our attention to questions like these:

What is it to be a child?
How do children's ways of thinking differ from "ours"?
Do young children have the capacity to be really altruistic?
Might it be that children have the right to "divorce" their parents?
Might some works of child art be artistically or aesthetically as good as "stick figures" or blotches of paint by some famous modern artist?
Does literature that is written by adults for children have to be, for that very reason, inauthentic?

I can remember resisting Mat's suggestion at first, but I soon came to accept it. In 1985, and again in 1988, I directed an NEH Summer Seminar for College Teachers under the title "Issues in the Philosophy of Childhood." I chose the title carefully. Wishing to avoid the task of proving to the National Endowment for the Humanities that the philosophy of childhood is, indeed, a legitimate subject for academic enquiry analogous to the philosophy of mind, the philosophy of mathematics, and the rest, I made as if I were simply selecting issues for discussion from an already accepted field of enquiry.

None of the twelve participants in each of those two seminars seemed to have any difficulty in accepting the idea that the philosophy of childhood should be recognized as a legitimate field of inquiry. We began our time together by thinking about our concept of childhood, a concept which turns out to be historically and culturally, as well as philosophically, problematic.

Our concept of childhood is historically problematic in that the notion we have of childhood may be a modern invention.[1] In earlier periods children seem to have been recognized as "little people," who, of course eat less and can do less work than "big people," but who may not be thought to differ in the *kinds* of tasks they can be assigned or in the *ways* they think or behave.

The concept of childhood is culturally problematic in that it is not shared fully by all other cultures. Margaret Mead tells about a Pacific Island culture in which stories are thought to be for adults, but not for children. Far from being a world of fantasy and imagination, childhood, in this culture, is a time of realistic and prosaic thought.[2]

Finally, the concept of childhood is philosophically problematic in that genuinely philosophical difficulties stand in the way of saying just what *kind* of difference the difference between children and adult human beings is.

We moved on in those two NEH Seminars to take up some of the topics that will occupy the succeeding chapters of this book. We talked about the ways that are available for understanding what it is to be a child, including the theory that the development of each human being recapitulates the history of the development of the human species (see Chapter 2). We discussed theories of cognitive development in children, especially the developmental theory of Jean Piaget (see Chapters 3 and 4). And we considered theories of moral development (see Chapter 5). We discussed art *by* children (Chapter 10) and literature *for* children (Chapter 9). And, of course, we debated children's rights (Chapter 6).

In fact, of the topics to be taken up in the following chapters, it is only Childhood Amnesia (Chapter 7) that was not an explicit part of our agenda. But even that subject slipped in occasionally with some remark to the effect that part of what makes early childhood so mysterious and so intriguing is that none of us can remember having been a very young child.

So I have been won over to Matthew Lipman's suggestion. It now seems to me quite clear that childhood, including the ideas and theories that people have about it, are, indeed, worthy of philosophical examination and critique. And I have taught my first course, at Mount Holyoke College, under the title "The Philosophy of Childhood."

In this book I do not try to give a full account of what might be included in this new subject, the philosophy of childhood. Instead, I present a personal response to some of the issues that belong to it. But in presenting *a* philosophy of childhood, indeed, something of *my own* philosophy of childhood, I hope to help secure a place in the philosophy curriculum of the future for *the* philosophy of childhood as a genuine area of academic research, writing, and teaching.

1

A Philosopher's View of Childhood

"Do you think there could be any such thing as the beginning of time?" I asked the dozen third and fourth graders in my philosophy discussion group in Newton, Massachusetts. (We had been trying to write a story about time travel.)

"No," several of the kids replied.

Then Nick spoke up. "The universe is everything and everywhere," he announced, and then paused. "But then if there was a big bang or something, what was the big bang *in*?"

Nick's question had long puzzled me, too. In my own case, hearing lectures on the "big bang" theory of the origin of the universe given by learned astrophysicists and cosmogonists had never quelled the conceptual worry that Nick articulated so simply and directly.

At the time of this discussion Nick had just turned nine years old. The others in the group were anywhere from nine to ten and a half.

Not only did Nick have a genuine puzzle about how the universe could have begun, he also had a metaphysical principle that required beginnings for everything, the universe included. Everything there is, he said, has a beginning. As he realized, that principle reintroduces the problem about the universe. "How did the universe start?" he kept asking.

"The universe," said Sam, "is what everything appeared *on*. It's not really anything. It's what other things started *on*."

"So there always has to be a universe?" I asked.

"Yeah," agreed Sam, "there always has to be a universe."

"So if there was always a universe," I went on, "there was no first time, either."

"There was a first time for certain things," explained Sam, "but not for the universe. There was a first time for the earth, there was a first time for the stars, there was a first time for the sun. But there was no first time for the universe."

"Can you convince Nick that the universe has to always be there?" I asked Sam.

Sam replied with a rhetorical question. "What would the universe have appeared *on*?" he asked simply.

"That's what I don't understand," admitted Nick.

Sam's conception of the universe (what everything else appears "on") is reminiscent of Plato's idea of the "receptacle" in his dialogue *Timaeus*: ". . . the mother and receptacle of all created and visible and in any way sensible things is not to be termed earth or air or fire or water, or any of their compounds, or any of the elements from which these are derived, but is an invisible and formless being which receives all things . . ." (*Timaeus* 51A). On this view the universe itself never came to be; it is what other things come to be in, or "on." If, as Ross, another child in the same group, put the point later in our discussion, things "started out on vast blackness, then that's just the universe then; the universe *is* vast blackness."

I have said that Sam's conception is reminiscent of Plato's. But there is a respect in which Sam's idea may be superior to Plato's. The idea of a receptacle is the idea of a container. A container walls some things in and other things out. To wall things in and out it must have walls. Sam's idea of what other things appear "on" projects three-dimensional reality onto two dimensions, but it allows us to think of the "ground of being" as having indefinite borders. Whether the universe is finite or infinite can be left indeterminate. By contrast, Plato's receptacle must be finite. Moreover, we must wonder what the nature of the receptacle's walls could be, though there is no answer to this question in Plato.

In our discussion Nick never gave up his principle that everything there is has a beginning. But he remained puzzled about how this principle could be applied to the universe itself. Every time he was asked what the universe could have first appeared on, he replied with engaging candor, "That's the part I don't get." Of course it was he who first raised this problem with his principle that everything there is has a beginning.

Many people are familiar with Saul Steinberg's *New Yorker* cover depicting the New Yorker's view of the country. Manhattan Island dominates the scene; the other boroughs of New York City are prominent, though smaller than Manhattan. San Francisco is to be seen in the distance at the other coast. And there is not much in between.

A philosopher's view of childhood is likely to be just as distorted. On the philosopher's view, children sit around conducting virtuoso discussions of mind-bending questions like 'Did the universe itself have a beginning, and if so, what did it begin on?' Although I have tried to document in my writings the claim that *some* children *sometimes* do this, even I would have to admit that this sort of activity is not the most obvious feature of childhood.

Still, it is worth pointing out that discussions such as the one I have just recorded can, and sometimes do, occur. There are at least two reasons why it is important to point this out. First, philosophical thinking in children has been left out of the account of childhood that developmental psychologists have given us. Even if philosophical thinking is far from the most prominent feature of childhood, its presence should be duly noted. For one thing, leaving it out encourages undeserved condescension toward children. If the most daunting intellectual challenges that Sam and Nick face are to learn the twelve-times table and the passive form of the verb "to be," condescension toward these children as thinkers has some warrant in fact. But if Sam and Nick can raise for us in vivid and compelling form the puzzles of how the universe could have begun, then there are at least some contexts in which they should be considered our partners in a joint effort to understand it all.

There is a second reason why it is important to take due account of philosophical thinking in young children. Doing so helps us understand philosophy.

Much of philosophy involves giving up adult pretensions to know. The philosopher asks, "What is time, anyway?" when other adults assume, no doubt unthinkingly, that they are well beyond the point of needing to ask that question. They may want to know whether they have enough time to do the week's shopping, or to pick up a newspaper. They may want to know what time it is, but it doesn't occur to them to ask, "What is time?" St. Augustine put the point well: "What, then, is time? Provided that no one asks me, I know. But if I want to explain it to a questioner, I am baffled" (*Confessions* 11.14). Among the annoying questions that children ask are some that are genuinely baffling. In important part, philosophy is an adult attempt to deal with the genuinely baffling questions of childhood.

I can't remember asking myself, as a child, what time is. But I did puzzle over the beginning of the world. My puzzlement as a child of five or six took the form of the following question: 'Supposing that God created the world at some particular time, how is it that the world looks as though it had been going on forever?'

I know now that my problem in cosmogony was a bit like that of St. Thomas Aquinas. Like me, Aquinas accepted the Christian doctrine that God created the world, indeed, created it, Aquinas supposed, out of nothing. (I don't know now whether the *ex nihilo* part belonged to my theology as a six-year-old.) But Aquinas was also very respectful of Aristotle's arguments for the eternity of the world. He had, then, somehow, to reconcile the appearance of beginninglessness, as captured in Aristotle's rather impressive reasoning, with the revealed doctrine of creation, which, he thought, was an absolute beginning.

For myself—that childhood self—I came up with an analogy. Having posed my question to my mother and received no helpful response, I returned later to reassure her. "Don't worry, Mom," I said, "I think it's like a perfect circle someone has drawn. If you had been there when it was drawn, you would know where the circle begins. But as you look at it now, there's no way of telling. It's like a perfect circle, where the end connects up with the beginning without showing."

When now, sixty years later, I teach Aristotle or Aquinas to university students, I try to locate the questioning child in me and my students. Unless I do so, the philosophy we do together will lose much of its urgency and much of its point.

Let's return to the point about respecting children as partners in inquiry. Parents and teachers are often so impressed with the burdens they bear in having to nurture, instruct, reassure, and inspire their children that they fail to appreciate what children have to offer adults. One of the exciting things that children have to offer us is a new philosophical perspective.

Consider the case of Kristin, who was four years old. She was teaching herself to use watercolors. As she painted, she began to think about the colors themselves. Sitting on her bed, talking to her father, she announced, "Dad, the world is all made of colors."

Kristin's father, who, as I happen to know, wants to make sense of it all as much as his four-year-old daughter did, liked Kristin's hypothesis, and reacted positively. But, recognizing a difficulty, he asked her, "What about glass?"

Kristin thought for a moment. Then she announced firmly, "Colors *and* glass."

Like any good philosopher, Kristin knew what to do when one's grand hypothesis runs into a counterexample. One simply incorporates the counterexample into the hypothesis!

Kristin's color hypothesis is not only fresh and exciting—at least as uniquely wonderful a gift to her father, I should say, as any one of the watercolor pictures she might have presented to him—it also recalls the thinking of the earliest philosophers we have any record of, the ancient Milesians. Like Kristin, the Milesians wanted to know what everything is made of. Thales said "Water" (presumably he thought that the earth was something like frozen or compacted water, and that air was very rarefied steam); Anaximander said "The infinite" or "The indefinite"; whereas Anaximines said "Air." (I like Kristin's hypothesis better than any of these.)

A later anecdote from Kristin recalls another pre-Socratic philosopher, Parmenides. Kristin was five, and learning how to read. She was learning to recognize syllables and to sound them out so as to be able to recognize words. She was quite proud of her success.

Again, sitting on her bed talking to her father, she commented, "I'm sure glad we have letters."

Kristin's father was somewhat surprised at that particular expression of gratitude. "Why?" he asked.

"Cause if there was no letters, there would be no sounds," explained Kristin. "If there was no sounds, there would be no words . . . If there was no words, we couldn't think . . . and if we couldn't think, there would be no world."

Kristin's chain reasoning is breathtaking. It is also reminiscent of Parmenides' enigmatic fragment *to gar auto noein estin te kai einai* ("For the same thing is there both to be thought of and to be"). That might be understood to entail 'Only what can be thought, can be.' If, then, we grant Kristin her interesting assumptions that (1) without words nothing could be thought and (2) without letters there would be no words, we get the fascinating conclusion 'Without letters there could be no world.'

Both these anecdotes from Kristin show how the thought of a

child may be a priceless gift to a parent or teacher with ears to hear. And both of them also give us reason to think of philosophy as, in part, an adult response to the questions of childhood.

The twentieth century has seen an amazing growth in the study of childhood. Two ideas have been central to the way childhood has been studied in our time. One is the idea that children develop and that their development is a *maturational* process. In part, maturation is, quite obviously, a biological process. Children grow bigger, their legs and arms grow longer, baby faces grow into older-looking faces, baby teeth fall out and are replaced by adult teeth, and so on. But maturation is also a psychological and social process. Baby talk, baby thoughts, and baby behavior are replaced by the talk, thoughts, and behavior of young children, then by that of older children, adolescents, and, finally, adults.

The second idea central to the recent study of childhood is that growth takes place in identifiable *stages*. As school teachers can testify, the stages of biological growth children experience can be correlated only roughly with their actual ages. Thus one child in a given class will tower over the rest, while another has yet to catch up with the class average. But the stages of biological, as well as intellectual and social, growth are at least broadly related to age. Putting the idea of maturation and the idea of a sequence of age-related stages together, we get the conception of child development as a maturational process with identifiable stages that fall into an at least roughly age-related sequence.

Clearly maturation has a goal; its goal is maturity. Early stages are superseded by later stages that are automatically assumed to have been less satisfactory. Thus the "stage/maturational model" of child development, as we can call it, which has found unquestioned acceptance in the study of childhood, has an evaluational bias built into it. Whatever the biological or psychological structures in a standard twelve-year-old turn out to be, the stage/maturational model of development guarantees, before any research is done at all, that these structures will be more nearly satisfactory than the superseded structures of, say, a six-year-old.

In many areas of human development this evaluational bias seems quite appropriate. We don't want grown-ups, or even adolescents, to have to chew their adult-sized steaks with baby teeth. But when it comes to philosophy, the assumption is quite out of place. There are several reasons for this.

First, there is no reason whatsoever to suppose that, simply by virtue of growing up in some standard way, adolescents or adults naturally achieve an appropriate level of maturity in handling philosophical questions—in, for example, being able to discuss whether time might have had a beginning, or whether some supercomputer might be said to have a mind.

Second, it should be obvious to anyone who listens to the philosophical comments and questions of young children that these comments and questions have a freshness and inventiveness that is hard for even the most imaginative adult to match. Freshness and inventiveness are not the only criteria for doing philosophy well: discipline and rigor should also count heavily. And children can be expected to be less disciplined and less rigorous than their adult counterparts. Still, in philosophy, as in poetry, freshness and inventiveness are much to be prized.

I recently asked a college class to respond, in writing, to Tim's question from the beginning of *Philosophy and the Young Child*: "Papa, how can we be sure that everything is not a dream?" A mother in my class recalled that her daughter, then three and a half, had once asked, "Mama, are we 'live' or are we on video?" This child's question obviously bears an important resemblance to the traditional dream question. But it is also a delightfully fresh and new question, one that could not have been conceived before TV, indeed before the development of video cameras and VCRs.

Some features of the dream problem carry over into the video problem. Thus just as I might have had the thought, in my dream, that I am awake, so the word "live" might appear on the screen when I am watching a video. But some features are new. Unlike the dream problem, the video problem suggests that our lives are already on tape, just waiting to be shown.

So children are often fresh and inventive thinkers. All too often, maturity brings with it staleness and uninventiveness. This is a second reason for rejecting the evaluational assumption built into the stage/maturational model of child development.

Third, Descartes taught us to do philosophy by "starting over." Instead of assuming the correctness of what my teachers have taught me, or what the society around me seems to accept, I am to make a fresh beginning to see if I can show by some means of my very own that I really do know whatever it is I claim to know. As college students soon learn in their first philosophy course, it isn't easy to rid oneself of adult assumptions, even temporarily, and even for a fairly circumscribed purpose. It isn't easy, that is, for adults. Children have far less of a problem. In a certain way, then, adult philosophers who follow Descartes in trying to "start over" are trying to make themselves as little children again, even if only temporarily. That is hard for adults. It is unnecessary for children.

It isn't that "starting over" is all there is to doing philosophy. That isn't true at all. But learning to be comfortable with "naive" questions is an important part of doing philosophy well. Thus for this reason, as well as for the other two, when it comes to doing philosophy, the evaluational assumption of the stage/maturational model gets things all wrong.

Like the New Yorker's view of the United States, my view of children as little philosophers is a distortion. But so also is the conventional view of childhood as a development through a sequence of roughly age-related stages that aims at maturity. Sometimes, it seems, the best way to correct one distortion is to pair it with an appealing, but opposed, distortion. I hope that that is true in this case.

2

Theories and Models of Childhood

Like many parents of our generation, my wife and I raised our children with a tattered copy of Benjamin Spock's *Baby and Child Care* close at hand. When a child's fever shot up in the middle of the night, it was comforting to find Dr. Spock saying, "Between the ages of 1 and 5 years, children may develop fever as high as 104°." And when a neighbor's child, at six months, still had no teeth, it was reassuring to be able to read to the neighbor from Dr. Spock, "One baby gets his first tooth at 3 months, another not till a year. Yet both are healthy, normal infants."[1]

At the beginning of the chapter titled "Your Baby's Development," however, Dr. Spock adopts a somewhat different tone. It is as if he were leaning back in his swivel chair and expatiating on grander themes. Section 351, which begins this chapter, carries the bold-print caption, "He's repeating the whole history of the human race." This first paragraph continues:

> There's nothing in the world more fascinating than watching a child grow and develop. At first you think of it as just a matter of growing bigger. Then, as he begins to do things, you may think of it as "learning tricks." But it's really more complicated and full of meaning than that. Each child as he develops is retracing the whole history of mankind, physically and spiritually, step by step. A baby starts off in the womb as a single tiny cell, just the way the first living thing appeared in the ocean. Weeks later, as he lies in the

amniotic fluid in the womb, he has gills like a fish. Toward the end of his first year of life, when he learns to clamber to his feet, he's celebrating that period millions of years ago when man's ancestors got up off all fours. It's just at that time that the baby is learning to use his fingers with skill and delicacy. Our ancestors stood up because they had found more useful things to do with their hands than walking on them. The child in the years after 6 gives up part of his dependence on his parents. He makes it his business to find out how to fit into the world outside his family. He takes seriously the rules of the game. He is probably reliving that stage of human history when our wild ancestors found it was better not to roam the forest in independent family groups but to form larger communities. (229)

Here Dr. Spock draws on something well beyond his own clinical experience, indeed, well beyond the clinical experience of any other physician, to present a theory of childhood. His theory is the recapitulation theory. It is captured in the slogan "Ontogeny recapitulates phylogeny," that is, the development of the individual repeats the development of the race or species.

Elements of the recapitulation theory can be traced back to the pre-Socratic philosophy of ancient Greece. But it was not until the nineteenth century that someone (the German biologist Ernst Haeckel) gave the theory a sophisticated modern formulation. A little later the American psychologist G. Stanley Hall, in his classic work *Adolescence*, gave the theory one of its most influential statements. Other modern thinkers who have given some credence to the theory include Freud, Piaget, and Karl Marx's collaborator, Friedrich Engels—not to mention Dr. Benjamin Spock![2]

We seem to know what Dr. Spock is doing when he gives us advice about teething, or about how high we can let the baby's temperature go before we get help. But what is he doing when he presents a theory of childhood?

Again, we can accept or reject Dr. Spock's advice about feeding or toilet training. It may go against our own experience, or against the advice of someone else we trust. But what might lead us to accept, or reject, Dr. Spock's recapitulation theory of childhood? For that matter, why do we need a theory of childhood in the first place? And what difference might it make whether we accept the one Dr. Spock promotes, or some other theory, or none at all?

Before I try to say a little in answer to these questions, I want to reflect for a moment on the naturalness with which we accept the idea that we need a good theory of childhood. I once visited a very good middle school to talk with teachers there about the possibility that they might do philosophy with their children. During the discussion one of the teachers asked me what the thinking of fourth graders was like. At first I thought this teacher was testing me. I thought that, knowing well himself what the thinking of fourth graders was like, he wanted to see if I knew, too. However, I soon had to reject that hypothesis.

After I had made one or two tentative comments, the situation suddenly struck me as ludicrous. The man who had asked the question was a very experienced teacher of fourth-grade children, whereas I had never in my life taught the fourth grade, or indeed, elementary school at any level. True, each of my own children had, by that time, passed through the fourth grade, and I had occasionally had philosophical discussions with small groups of elementary school children, including fourth graders. But by any reasonable measure I had had relatively little experience with the children this experienced fourth-grade teacher was asking me about. If anything, *he* was the expert, and certainly the profes-sional; I was the novice, the amateur. Why should I, a teacher of university students, be able to tell him about the thinking of the very creatures he spent his working days with, when I saw them only very occasionally?

I think the answer is that this teacher had become used to the idea that university professors have *theories* about children—about how they think, how they behave, and what they are like *at this stage or that.* He was so used to the idea of experts' theories that he was quite prepared to suppose that some outsider from a university somewhere might be able to tell him what the people he knew best were really like.

It is, no doubt, mostly to psychologists that we look these days for theories of childhood. But educators, too, have theories, as do anthropologists and even language theorists, not to mention cultural historians and political scientists. Might a philosopher have anything useful to say about theories of childhood?

As I have already admitted, philosophers have been, on the whole, remarkably silent on the question of what a child is. But it would be rash to conclude from this that philosophy has nothing to contribute to the theoretical discussion of childhood. Philosophy in the past has been preoccupied with problematic concepts like space, time, causality, God, free will, and the like. As it turns out, the concept of a child is also problematic in ways that are philosophical.

The simplest theory as to what a child is we could call "the little person theory of childhood." According to that theory, a child is just a very small, because very young, human being. This is the theory one might accept when one thinks of child development as enlargement. As Dr. Spock puts it, "At first you think of [development] as just a matter of growing bigger."

Clearly there is, usually, a significant size difference between children and other human beings. Children are generally larger than infants, but smaller than adolescents and adults. This observation is not quite as innocuous as it might at first seem. It means that children, unlike most of the rest of us, are typically surrounded by "giants," some of whom bend over to converse with them, or even sit on the floor to be more on a level with them, but most of whom are content to enjoy their position of lofty superiority.

Much of the manufactured world around children is not appropriate to their size. Children may not be able to reach the light switch, or even the doorknob, let alone the door knocker (or the cookie jar!). The message this gives to children is unmistakable: "You are not (yet) a full member of society."

A child's size, moreover, is constantly changing. In fact, the topic of size is a common subject for adult remarks to and about children. "My, how you have grown!" says the adult, as the child squirms. In this respect children are quite unlike most adults. Adults may put on weight, or get pregnant, or go gray and wrinkled, and men, especially, may lose their hair. But for an adult it is in general okay, and sometimes even good, to be recognized, even after a long interval, as "looking just the same." A child, by contrast, is always in transition, and most obviously with respect to size. Children shouldn't continue to look just the same. They need to grow up. As a matter of natural course, this year's pants will soon be too short and last year's shoes have already been outgrown.

In the whimsical children's story *The Shrinking of Treehorn*, the hero, Treehorn, begins shrinking instead of growing.[3] Treehorn's parents and teachers give Treehorn the clear message that he is doing something wrong. He is failing to grow up as normal children do.

Children who grow faster than their age peers, or more slowly, are often made to feel that there is something wrong, even that they are *doing* something wrong. Not only is children's size thus in transition; there is also a normal *rate* of change.

So far, then, a child is a small, growing human being—bigger than an infant, but smaller than an adolescent. Is that all? How do we make our theory of childhood more interesting, and more complex?

We need to take account of development that is not just enlargement. In particular, we need to take account of cognitive, emotional, and social development.

Philosophers in the seventeenth century debated whether the

most important ideas we have as adults are innate, or whether they arise from experience we have had since infancy. The rationalists, like René Descartes, were innatists; the empiricists, like John Locke, were experientialists. Here is a passage in which Descartes speculates on the thinking of a fetus in its mother's womb:

> This does not mean that I believe that the mind of an infant meditates on metaphysics in its mother's womb; . . . it seems most reasonable to think that a mind newly united to an infant's body is wholly occupied in perceiving or feeling the ideas of pain, pleasure, heat, cold and other similar ideas which arise from its union and intermingling with the body. Nonetheless, it has in itself the ideas of God, itself, and all such truths as are called self-evident, in the same way as adult humans have when they are not attending to them; it does not acquire these ideas later on, as it grows older.

Here is Locke, taking the experientialist side:

> Let us then suppose the mind to be, as we say, white paper, void of all characters, without any ideas:—How comes it to be furnished? Whence comes it by that vast store which the busy and foundless fancy of man has painted on it with an almost endless variety? Whence has it all the *materials* of reason and knowledge? To this I answer, in one word, from EXPERIENCE.[4]

The debate between innatism and experientialism has continued down to the present time, though the terms of reference have shifted somewhat. Today the leading experientialists are behaviorists, the most famous being B. F. Skinner. Behaviorists differ from Locke in that they forswear all interest in the contents of our minds. They view the mind as a "black box," rather than a "white paper" on which experience "writes." According to behaviorists, the way experience "writes" on human and other animal organisms is through operant conditioning. Or, to shift to another metaphor, "Operant conditioning shapes behavior as a sculptor shapes a lump of clay."[5]

The most prominent innatist of our time is the linguist Noam

Chomsky, who supposes that all of us are born with the structures of a universal grammar "wired in." The flavor of Chomsky's approach can be appreciated by noting what he has to say about what he calls "Plato's problem," that is, the problem of explaining how we can know as much as we do when the evidence available to us is so limited. "Much of the interest of the study of language, in my opinion," Chomsky writes,

> lies in the fact that it offers an approach to Plato's problem in a domain that is relatively well circumscribed and open to inspection and inquiry, and at the same time deeply integrated in human life and thought. If we can discover something about the principles that enter into the construction of this particular cognitive system, the principles of the language faculty, we can progress toward a solution for at least one special and quite important case of Plato's problem. We can then ask whether these principles generalize to other cases . . . My own belief is that the principles . . . are in crucial respects specific to the language faculty, but that the approach may indeed be suggestive elsewhere . . .[6]

Suppose we reserve the term 'innatist' for people who, like Chomsky, think that the most basic cognitive structures do not evolve during the development of a human individual, though of course those structures may go from being *merely latent* to becoming *manifest*. Then we can make a fairly clean distinction between innatists and recapitulationists. For the recapitulationists the structures themselves are like Japanese flowers: they unfold during childhood. Moreover, the way in which they unfold repeats the way the human race has evolved and developed in history.

What difference does it make whether one is an experientialist, an innatist, or a recapitulationist about childhood? First off, we must admit that no one today is in a position to present an altogether adequate theory of childhood that would command the respect of developmental psychologists, anthropologists, linguists, and educational theorists. What we have instead are a number of theoretical models that guide research in more limited ways and offer help in interpreting data. Some of these models fit neatly under the innatist, the experientialist, or the recapitulationist banner. Others fall under more than one category, or combine aspects of one orientation with something else, say, a theory of sexuality or a theory of human personality. Thus Piaget, for example, tries to combine all three of the models I have mentioned,[7] and Freud combines a recapitulationist model with his own theory of human sexuality.[8]

Theoretical models have the virtue of suggesting connections we might not have made without them. But as long as we have alternative models, each useful in its own way but none clearly and obviously superior to all the rest, we should be on the lookout for what a given model may encourage us to overlook, or misunderstand, as well as for what that model may help us understand better.

Consider the recapitulation model, with which we began. By appeal to the recapitulation model Dr. Spock encourages us to become fascinated with the way our baby grows and develops by thinking of that infant as "retracing the whole history of mankind, physically and spiritually, step by step." That is not a bad way to celebrate the growth and development of one's child.

The recapitulation model may be suggestive and helpful to the scientific researcher as well as to the parent. Elizabeth Bates, in her article "The Emergence of Symbols: Ontogeny and Phylogeny," explains how certain "component parts" of language (imitation, tool use, social motivation to share reference to objects) may have evolved separately in phylogeny and how developments in the infant just before language acquisition may be thought of as recapitulating the evolutionary sequence.[9]

It is, by contrast, the experientialist model that lies behind recent research showing that babies learn to discriminate the basic sounds of the language they hear around them even before they reach six months of age. According to this research babies who regularly hear English spoken in their presence are able to distinguish the sounds 'la' and 'ra' at six months, whereas babies who have heard Japanese instead are not.[10]

The innatist model guides other research in fruitful directions. In a paper called "Cognitive Basis of Language Learning in Infants" John Macnamara offers evidence that "infants learn their language by first determining, independent of language, the meaning which a speaker intends to convey to them, and by then working out the relationship between the meaning and the expression they heard." To be able to do this, Macnamara supposes, the infants must already have, wired into their neurology, a mental language. It is this innate "mentalese" that then gets expressed, he thinks, in the acquired, natural language—English, say, or Norwegian, or Chinese.[11]

There is another moral I wish to stress even more than the one about theoretical guidance. Children are not only objects of study; they are also, with us, members of what Kant called "the kingdom of ends." It is all right to be curious about them, and we should certainly feel responsibility for their education and welfare; but, above all, we owe them respect. And here is precisely where our theoretical models for understanding them may dehumanize them and encourage inappropriately condescending attitudes toward them.

Consider these recapitulationist sentiments of Carl Gustav Jung: "Childhood, however, is a state of the past . . . The child lives in a pre-rational and above all in a pre-scientific world, the world of people who existed before us."[12] A cause for concern here is the claim that children live in a pre-rational and pre-scientific world. That claim must be treated with great caution. Whereas it is certainly good to be warned that a child's ideas may, in a given context, be quite different from yours or mine, to maintain that children live in a pre-scientific and even pre-rational world is arrogant and inappropriately condescending.

For one thing, a young child may understand something about

the modern, scientific world better than most adults do. Take computers, or just video games. When the neighbor children from up the lane come to visit me, they sometimes bring their pocket video games with them. They try to explain to me what is happening when their little fingers press the keys on the keyboard so nimbly and effectively, but alas, they don't usually succeed. I am the one, I feel, who belongs to the pre-scientific world—certainly to the pre-video-game world!

As for the thought of children's being pre-rational, Piaget, perhaps more than anyone else, has shown us in dramatic ways how the responses of children may sometimes seem bafflingly irrational. (We shall explore that topic further in Chapter 4.) But sometimes children are also surprisingly rational, even wise. Consider the following example.

Some years ago a young mother came up to me after a talk I had given to tell me about taking her four-year-old son to see his grandfather, who was dying. The boy could see that the grandfather was in a bad way. (He died a week later.) On the way home the boy said to his mother, "When people are sick and ready to die, like Grandpa, do they shoot them?" The mother was shocked. "No," she replied, "the police wouldn't like that." (Here the mother's response was something Lawrence Kohlberg would put at a pre-moral stage of moral development; see Chapter 5.)

The boy thought a bit more and then said, "Maybe they could just do it with medicine."

It is quite possible that this four-year-old had seen or heard of some seriously ill or maimed pet or farm animal that was, as we say, "put out of its misery" by being shot. Why not Grandpa? The analogy is apt. It is part of what moves doctors to administer lethal doses to dying patients who are in misery; it is part of what moves many of us to agree that euthanasia, in certain circumstances, may be ethically acceptable, even ethically obligatory.

There is, in principle, no limit to the sophistication one may bring to the discussion of euthanasia. One can certainly invoke moral theories and moral principles that one would not be able to explain to that four-year-old child. However, I suspect that most actual cases of euthanasia in our culture are conceived and carried out in terms that would be perfectly intelligible to that young child. If I am right, then this case counts as evidence against the recapitulationist idea that the child must live in a pre-rational world.

There may, of course, be very good reasons why that child's mother would not want to discuss euthanasia with him. But "He wouldn't understand" is not one of them. The recapitulationist model, insofar as it suggests that a four-year-old would necessarily be unable to understand what motivates a caring physician to give a lethal dose to a dying patient, or a caring daughter to consent to that act, gives us a bad reason for invoking what Kohlberg calls the "punishment-and-obedience orientation" and cutting off all discussion of the ethical issues involved in dealing with dying loved ones.

The models of development that theories of childhood offer to stimulate our research and challenge our attempts at understanding children may have many useful functions. But we must guard against letting those models caricature our children and limit the possibilities we are willing to recognize in our dealings with them as fellow human beings.

3

Piaget and Philosophy

Jean Piaget had a very special kind of genius. He was able to think up experiments with these three crucial characteristics:

First, they have *arresting* results. They show children reacting to experimental situations in ways that surprise us because they are so very different from the ways in which *we* would react.

Two balls of clay that, as the child agrees, contain the same amount of clay are flattened—the one drastically, the other minimally. "Are they still the same?" asks the experimenter, cagily. "No," says the child, obligingly. Then, pointing to the thicker one, the child adds, "That one is heavier."

We are startled by such results. We become intrigued. Second, the experiments are *replicable*. Piaget's most famous experiments, such as those concerning conservation, are, in fact, fairly easy to replicate. You don't need fancy equipment. You don't need to choose "the right children"; most any children will do. You *do* need to ask the children exactly what Piaget asked—or at least you need to come as close as your own language will allow. But you don't need complicated scoring manuals to record the results, let alone special training sessions to be able to observe what is going on.

Third, the experiments reveal an *age-related sequence*. It matters how old the children are, and, in general, if you bring back the same children a couple of years later—almost regardless of what has happened in the meantime, so long as Mother Time has ticked away for a couple of years—the children will react differently. With only the slightest encouragement from Piaget we can see from the experiments that the children are now *at a different stage.*

Only a first-rate genius could think of lots of experiments that all, or almost all, have these three features. These three features, by themselves, go a very long way toward selling us on Piaget's theory. Perhaps better: these very general features of Piaget's experiments are pretty much enough to sell most people on the general idea of a Piagetian theory of cognitive development, with really very little regard for what the detailed content of that theory turns out to be. Note how this is so.

First, the fact that the experiments produce arresting results easily convinces us that, knowing our children so well, we don't in fact know them at all. It convinces us that our children are, in important ways, strangers to us. It's not enough, we quickly conclude, to be with our children all day long to get to know them. We need a *theory* about them. The expert, the theoretician, needs to tell us parents and teachers what our children are really like. Piaget's arresting experiments bring home that message.

No doubt the fourth-grade teacher I mentioned in the last chapter who asked me, "What's the thought of fourth graders like?" had received that message. *He* was the fourth-grade teacher. *I* was the college professor. He spent his whole day with fourth graders. I didn't. Yet he wanted *me* to tell him what these creatures he spent his whole day with were like, or anyway, what their thought was like. Perhaps somewhere in his teacher training he had learned, and been influenced by, Piaget's arresting experiments. Perhaps for that reason he was open to being told by some supposed expert that the thought processes of the very children he saw every day were really very different from anything his regular exposure to them would lead him to expect.

Second, the fact that these experiments are replicable makes it quite plausible to think there lurks a science in this vicinity. There must be, it seems, a scientific theory that these experiments confirm, a theory quite on a par with the theories that get confirmed by similarly replicable experiments in physics and chemistry that our colleagues in the natural sciences run every day.

Third, the fact that these experiments display an age-related sequence of results makes it virtually impossible to resist the conclusion that cognitive development is a *maturational* process, in fact a maturational process quite analogous to familiar processes of biological maturation. We know it is no good trying to teach a newborn infant to walk. The bones, muscles, and nervous system of the infant need to mature first. Similarly, it is overwhelmingly natural to conclude from Piaget's experiments that it's no good trying to teach kids anything except what is "age-appropriate." Mental bones and psychological muscles need to mature, too.

Without going into any detail in this chapter concerning Piaget's experiments, and without considering the specific content of the theories Piaget takes them to support, I want now to connect this general characterization of Piaget with a question that naturally arises from Chapter 1, namely, Is it worthwhile *encouraging* children to do philosophy? Consider first the maturational point, that is, the point that seems to be brought out by the age-related sequences of interestingly different responses to Piaget's questions. This point naturally prompts one to ask whether doing philosophy is a cognitively *mature* activity, or, instead, a cognitively *immature* activity. If it is a mature activity, then we shouldn't expect anyone who isn't cognitively mature to engage in it naturally. More particularly, we shouldn't expect to find that doing philosophy is a natural activity of childhood. Evidence, or apparent evidence, to the contrary—such as that presented in the first chapter—would be highly suspect. *Prima facie,* evidence to the contrary would have to be chalked up either to (1) overinterpreting the data, that is, reading philosophy into the words of young children, or else to (2) having an insufficient grasp of what real philosophy is, and hence mistaking only apparently philosophical comments and questions for the real thing.

As for actually encouraging children to do philosophy, if philosophy is a cognitively mature activity, to encourage children to do philosophy would be as pointless, perhaps even as damaging to the child, as trying to get newborn infants to walk. Doing philosophy would not be an "age-appropriate activity" for children, certainly not for young ones.

So much for assuming that doing philosophy is a cognitively mature activity. Alternatively one might try supposing that philosophy is a cognitively immature activity. In that case one would certainly expect to find children naturally engaged in doing philosophy all right, but then there would be no point in *encouraging* children in this, for it would be something the normal ones, anyway, could be expected to grow out of. (Professional philosophers like me would be children, who, in an important respect, simply never grew up.)

Now none of this fits either what we know about children or what we know about philosophy. Suppose philosophy is taken to be a cognitively mature activity, hence presumably not something either naturally found in children or appropriately to be encouraged in them. I have myself presented evidence, for example in *Philosophy and the Young Child*, that some young children do quite naturally make comments, ask questions, and even engage in reasoning that professional philosophers can recognize as philosophical. When Ian in that book, age six, protests to his mother that the three unpleasant children of his parents' visiting friends have taken over the TV set and kept him from watching his favorite program, he asks provocatively, "Why is it better for three people to be selfish than for one?" Deftly he turns on its head the utilitarian justification for that particular case of aggrandizement, namely, "Three people are being made *happy*, rather than just one."

Ian's question, even if motivated by rage and frustration, is philosophically acute. It is not proto-philosophical, or quasi-philosophical, or semi-philosophical; it is the real thing, the very same kind of probing and questioning that takes place among professional philosophers in their seminars, conferences, and informal discussions with one another (perhaps also, in some cases, motivated by rage or frustration, or by the need to get a job, rather than the pure love of wisdom).

I have also presented evidence, for example in *Dialogues with Children*, that even after children have been socialized out of doing philosophy naturally, say between the ages of eight and twelve, they respond beautifully to the opportunity to engage in philosophy when it is presented to them with some imagination. The remarkable success of the Philosophy for Children Program developed by Matthew Lipman and his colleagues provides much more substantial testimony to the same effect.

As for supposing that philosophy is a cognitively immature activity, that simply doesn't fit the reality. It is true that there is something characteristically naive about philosophy; but it is a profound naiveté, not a cognitively immature sort. Consider the Kristin anecdotes from the first chapter. In one, Kristin, age four, proposed the hypothesis "The world is all made of colors." In the second, Kristin, age five now, expressed gratitude for letters, "Cause if there was no letters, there would be no sounds; if there was no sounds, there would be no words; if there was no words, we couldn't think; and if we couldn't think, there would be no world." If that's *im*maturity, what's so great about maturity?

One way out of the awkward dilemma posed by asking whether doing philosophy is a cognitively mature or a cognitively immature activity is to say that sometimes it is one and sometimes the other. Piaget himself often suggested that children, in their cognitive development, recapitulate the history of Western philosophy. This recapitulationist idea belongs to the same family as the suggestion from Dr. Spock that I discussed in the last chapter. But it focuses on a, cosmically speaking, relatively recent period of history.

According to this suggestion, children begin by being little pre-Socratics.[1] They go on to become, successively, Platonists, Aristotelians, Scholastics, Cartesians, and then, perhaps, British empiricists. Now I myself don't think the evidence supports any such claim of general development. But suppose it did. The problem about maturity would not be solved, unless one supposed that the history of philosophy itself exhibits a maturational process. And surely there is inadequate reason to suppose that that is so. It would, I think, be quite easy to argue that on any reasonable scale of maturity, Plato was as mature a thinker as Quine, or Kripke, or Habermas, or Derrida.

To consider the Kristin anecdotes again, I have already suggested that there is at least some limited affinity between Kristin's idea that the world is made of colors and familiar ideas that the pre-Socratic Milesians—Thales, Anaximander, and Anaximenes—put forward about "world stuff." I have also suggested that we link Kristin's breathtaking reasoning about how without letters there would be no world to the later pre-Socratic philosopher Parmenides. After all, Parmenides said something like "The same thing can be thought as can be."

Yet even if we suppose Parmenides to have been a more mature thinker than the Milesians, there is an obvious way in which you simply don't get any more *mature* philosophically than someone who can say, "Without words there would be no thought and without thought there would be no world." That is remarkably close to absolute idealism; it's also close to modern deconstructionism. Kristin at twelve or twenty or forty-eight may well reject that line of reasoning, or, more likely, forget it and become interested in something else instead; but if she does any of those things, the explanation will not be that she has become a more *mature* thinker.

Frustrated with this problem of how to fit child philosophy into a story about cognitive development suggested by Piaget's arresting experiments, one might try saying that philosophy hasn't anything much to do with cognitive development at all. Perhaps the interest in doing philosophy and the ability to do it well occur in childhood quite independently of the capacities cognitive psychologists are interested in.

Of course we can make 'cognitive development' a technical term for whatever is revealed by Piaget's arresting experiments. And then it will be true, I think, that philosophy is somewhat peripheral to cognitive development—whatever cognitive development, so understood, turns out to be, that is, whatever the best account of those arresting experiments should turn out to be. (It might turn out, say, that those differential responses are largely a matter of progressive socialization. But I needn't take any stand on that question here.)

This last move invites the obvious question, Should we as parents and teachers be interested in philosophical thinking in young children, rather than just cognitive development—where cognitive development is now taken to be simply the Piagetian stuff? I myself think the answer is clearly yes. But whether or not I am right, we get no help from the now trivialized truth that philosophy has little to do with cognitive development.

Let's return to the fourth-grade teacher who took me aback by asking me, "What's the thought of fourth graders like?" I think he assumed I could tell him something interesting and worthwhile about the *stage* of cognitive development characteristic of fourth graders, maybe that I could recount some arresting experimental results in the fashion of Piaget and give him a little theory to help him make those arresting results intelligible to himself.

I may have left the impression earlier that I, as a philosopher, could certainly do no such thing. But in fact I think there is a service philosophers can render to nonphilosophical parents and teachers that is at least partially analogous to what the fourth-grade teacher wanted me to do for him.

Philosophers, in devoting their lives to the study of the profoundly naive questions of philosophy, can help nonphilosophical parents and teachers to recognize and appreciate some of the naively profound questions of childhood. It isn't that a philosopher can say, "At age five you can expect your daughter, if she is normal, to be concerned with the problem of the external world." Or, "At age seven you can expect your son, if he is developmentally on track, to be preoccupied with the problem of induction." What a professional philosopher can do is to collect examples of philosophical thinking in young children and then, by linking those childish thoughts to our philosophical tradition, help parents and teachers to recognize philosophy in their children, respect it when it appears, and even participate in it and encourage it on occasion.

Consider this anecdote from Christa Wolf's recent novel *Störfall*. The narrator is having a telephone conversation with her daughter about the daughter's son, a boy of presumably six or seven years of age. The boy's mother talks first, then the grandmother, who is also the book's narrator.

> "He roars around outside the whole day on his bicycle . . . Otherwise he occupies himself with the basic questions of existence. Today, for example, sitting on the potty he asked his father through the door, 'How does the big bathroom door get through my small eye?' "
>
> "For heaven's sake," I said; "and what happened then?"
>
> "Naturally his father produced a precise drawing for him: the bathroom door, the eye, in which the rays of light cross, the route through the optic nerve to the visual center in the brain, and that it is the business of the brain to enlarge the tiny image in the consciousness of the observer to the normal size of a bathroom door."
>
> "Well? Did that satisfy him?"
>
> "You know him. Do you know what he said?—'And how can I be certain that my brain really makes the bathroom door the right size?' "
>
> "Well," I said after a pause; "what do *you* think? How can we be certain?"
>
> "Stop it!" said my daughter; "not you, too!"[2]

Although this incident appears in a novel, it is almost surely based on a real-life event. Let's call the child, who is given no name in the story, Karl.

Karl's worry about how the bathroom door, which is big, can get through his eye, which is small, is a little like a worry my own son once had, a worry I reported on in *Philosophy and the Young Child* (8–9):

> I am tucking my eight-year-old son, John, in bed. He looks up at me and asks, quite without warning, "Daddy, why don't I see you double, because I have two eyes and I can see you with each one by itself?"
>
> What do I say?
>
> First, I try to make sure that I understand what is puzzling him. "You have two ears," I point out. "Are you surprised you don't *hear* double?"
>
> John grins. "What is hearing double?"
>
> "Well, maybe my-my voi-voice wo-would s-sound li-like thi-this," I say.
>
> He reflects. "But your ears both go to the same place."
>
> "And couldn't it be that your eyes both go to the same place?" I suggest.
>
> He gets serious, thinks, then grins again. "You're just giving me another problem," he protests. "I want to think about the one I already have."
>
> Fair enough. "Maybe," I suggest, "it's because the picture you get with your left eye comes together with the picture you get with your right eye. When they come together they make *one* picture."
>
> We experiment with two fingers, one closer to our eyes, the other farther away. We try focusing now on one, now on the other. The aim is to see how, by focusing on the nearer finger, we can see the farther one double and vice versa. The moral is supposed to be that the two pictures don't *always* come together to make one, though they usually do.
>
> My son is not satisfied. It turns out that he has constructed for

himself, elaborating in various ways on what he has learned at school about vision and the retinal image, a complex theory of vision according to which one image comes through each eye, is reversed, rereversed, and then projected in front of the subject. No wonder he is worried about why we don't see double!

I suggest several ways of simplifying his theory, but he won't accept simplifications.

"I'll have to think about it some more," he says. "I'll talk to you again after I get it worked out."

John's schoolteacher, like Karl's father, seems to have thought that the fact that we have retinal images explains how we can see. But, as philosophers from Descartes and Leibniz right down to the present day have pointed out, the fact that we have retinal images brings with it problems of its own. We have two retinal images, yet normally we don't see double. Why? (John) Or: Okay, so projecting an image onto the retina, in fact a *very small* image onto the retina, is how a big object like the bathroom door gets into something as small as an eye. But how can the brain use a tiny image to figure out what size things really are? Does it in fact generally figure out what size things really are? (Karl)

I don't think there is any age such that it is natural for children of that age to ask why it is that we don't generally see double. Nor do I think there is any standard age for children to ask how it is that the large objects one sees can get through the small opening in one's eye, or how we can be certain that one's brain makes the bathroom door seem the right size. Yet many young children do puzzle over vision, and many puzzle over it in a genuinely philosophical way.

In any case, Karl's questions, like John's, are an invitation to do philosophy. A parent or teacher who doesn't hear the questions, or doesn't understand that they are more than, and different from, a mere request for information, misses a chance to do philosophy. That parent or teacher also misses out on something interesting and important about Karl, and John, and other children like them. It is something Piaget's remarkable experiments will not help us much to appreciate. They may even stand in the way.

If I am right about all of this, or even some of it, then it is imperative that we not let the results of Piaget's genuinely remarkable experiments set our educational agenda or define for us the capacity for thought and reflection in our young children.

4

Piaget and Conservation

So far, no doubt, I could be charged with being a romantic about childhood. Perhaps I am a romantic. I admit that I want to encourage in adults—especially in college students who take my philosophy courses, but also in adults quite generally—a style of "naive" questioning that comes naturally to many children, and comes hard, often very hard, to many adults.

Piaget, one might think, is much more serious about childhood than I am. He realizes how important it is for children to grow up. He wants to help us all understand better some of the ways in which growing up, mentally, requires overcoming what one might call the "cognitive deficits" of childhood.

To sharpen up what I want to say about Piaget let us turn, now, to some of those supposed deficits and to the gains that are supposed to wipe them out. In this chapter I shall argue that even the cognitive developments that Piaget charts most persuasively are not the straightforward achievements they might at first seem to be.

Conservation experiments are perhaps the most famous experiments in the Piagetian repertory. They lie at the heart of his contribution to the study of childhood. They offer what he himself seems to have taken as crucial support for his claim that young children are what he calls "egocentric phenomenalists."

In this chapter I shall devote myself exclusively to what Piaget and his colleague Bärbel Inhelder say about the conservation of "substance," weight, and volume in young children. I shall take as my main text the canonical statement of Piaget's findings in this area, namely, Piaget and Inhelder, *The Child's Construction of Quantities: Conservation and Atomism.*[1]

Piaget and Inhelder report finding that children from five to thirteen years old react to (1) the deformation of a ball of clay, (2) the dissolution of lumps of sugar in a beaker of water, and (3) the popping of a grain of popcorn, in ways that can be organized into four main stages, three of which fall into substages as follows:

Stage I   —up to age 7 or 8
Stage II (A, then B)   —8 to 10
Stage III (A, then B)   —10 to 11 or 12
Stage IV (A, then B)   —12 and on

In the clay-ball experiments the children are first presented with clay in the shape of a ball; then, before their eyes, the ball is flattened, or twisted into a coil, or cut into pieces. Next, the children are asked, concerning the clay in its new deformed or minced condition: (i) Is there as much clay as before? (ii) Does the clay weigh as much as before? (iii) Will the clay displace as much water as before (that is, when dunked into a beaker, make the water go up as high as it did before)?

At Stage I the children answer no to all three questions—even when they have been shown the result of putting the deformed clay on a balance to reveal its weight, or into a marked beaker of water to reveal its volume. At Stage IIA children waver in answering (i) and then at IIB say yes to (i), but they continue to answer no to (ii) and (iii), again, despite what seems to us to be clear empirical evidence for a "yes" answer. At Stage IIIA children waver concerning (ii) and then at IIIB they answer yes to (ii) as well as (i), but they still answer no to (iii). At IVA there is a wavering response to (iii) and finally at IVB children answer yes to all three questions.

To their experiments with the clay ball Piaget and Inhelder add two more sets of experiments—one concerning lumps of sugar and once concerning a popcorn seed. Dependably at Stage IIB, and not at all before IIA, a child will suppose that the sugar persists in the water after the lumps have completely dissolved. Dependably at IIIB, and not at all before IIIA, the child will suppose the weight of the solution will be the same after the sugar has dissolved as before. And dependably at IVB, and not before IVA, the child will suppose the volume, as marked by the water level in the beaker, to remain the same after dissolution.

The experiments with the popcorn seed are similar, except for the Stage IVB response. At this stage, Piaget and Inhelder report, the child will suppose something very complicated, namely, that the sum of the volumes of the bits (atoms) that make up the popped popcorn seed will be the same as the sum of the volumes of the bits (atoms) that made up the unpopped grain. They will suppose this, Piaget and Inhelder report, even though they obviously realize that the gross volume of the seed is much greater after it has been popped than before.

In interpreting these results Piaget and Inhelder make such comments as these:

> . . . while the invariance of solid objects is acquired during the sensori-motor stage (beginning at the end of the first year of life), the conservation of matter, weight and volume is not constructed until a later phase of development. (3)

> The first stage marks a total failure to grasp the conservation of substance, weight and volume, even during very slight deformations in shape. (5)

> Stage II sees the discovery of the conservation of substance, but not yet of weight and volume. (9)

> Sub-Stage IIIB sees the immediate affirmation of the conservation of weight, conceived as a logical necessity. (42–43)

What exactly are the principles that, according to Piaget and Inhelder, are "constructed" or discovered during this development? They never say. It is a revealing commentary on their attitudes, both to the children they are studying and to the great metaphysical and scientific questions at issue in these experiments, that they never bother to formulate the principles the children seem to be laboring to discover, or, as they say, "to construct."

Consider the principle of the conservation of volume. The idea can't be simply that, say, the volume of a solid object is invariant through time. Balloons and popcorn would be obvious counterexamples. Is it that the sum of the volumes of the atoms that constitute a solid object is invariant through time? That won't do either. People and trees grow in volume, even in the sum of the volumes of their constituent atoms.

Is the idea rather that solid objects are conserved in substance, weight, and volume through *certain kinds of change*? But then we need to know through *what kinds* of change they are conserved. There is no discussion in Piaget and Inhelder of the kinds of change through which substance, weight, and volume are conserved.

Perhaps the best way of understanding what Piaget and Inhelder are after is to confine oneself to cases in which nothing is added to, or taken away from, a solid object or liquid mass. Following this idea, we might arrive at the following formulations of the relevant conservation principles (where 'CS' stands for conservation of substance, 'CW' for conservation of weight, and 'CV' for conservation of volume):

(CS) One will end up with just as much *stuff* as one started out with, so long as no *stuff* has been added or taken away.

(CW) One will end up with something that *weighs* exactly as much as it did at the beginning, so long as no stuff has been added or taken away.

(CV) One will end up with something that *displaces* exactly as much liquid as it did at the beginning (or, anyway, whose atoms col-

lectively displace exactly as much . . . as they did at the beginning), so long as no stuff has been added or taken away.

These are very nice principles indeed. When I say that they are
very nice, I don't mean to suggest that I accept them. I don't.
(More on that in a moment.) But, if Piaget and Inhelder are right,
I once did. Anyway, as I say, these are very nice principles. They
are intellectually very satisfying. They speak well of children as
natural philosophers.

What is going on when children gradually come to accept these
principles? Here is my own interpretation.

At Stage I, children have rather impressionistic notions of the
quantity of objects and masses. It may very well be, as Piaget and
Inhelder suggest, that a child will emphasize one dimension and
ignore the others. Thus a child might decide that a wad of clay,
in being elongated, had become "bigger" than it was before and
might decide this on the basis of length alone, ignoring thickness.

The move to Stage II is closely related to accepting the
combined principles (A) Nothing comes out of nothing, and
(B) Nothing passes away into nothing. Together, (A) and (B),
plus the assumption (C) Substance cannot be transformed into
anything that is not substance (for example, energy), yield the
principle that Piaget calls the conservation of substance (CS).

As for (CW), the chief notions of weight at Stages I and II seem
to be somewhat disorganized ideas of felt lightness and felt heav-
iness. There may, however, be other ideas, perhaps incompatible
ideas, as well, for example, the idea that a squashed ball of clay is
actually heavier than it was before because it presses down over a
bigger area. Using the dominant notions, though, the notions of
weight "to the feel," the child will naturally conclude that the clay
is lighter after the ball has been flattened and the popcorn lighter
after the grain has been popped.

What seems to happen at Stage III is that the child develops a
notion of weight that is linked to standard weighing procedures,

for example, to the use of a balance. With this new notion available, the child will reason that deformation and dissolution are, at some appropriate level of analysis, simply rearrangements of the bits that make things up. Since the weight of the whole, the reasoning continues, is the simple sum of the weights of the bits that make it up, neither deformation nor dissolution alters total weight.

At Stage IV children develop the notion of three-dimensional volume equivalence. (Before this stage they had been working with an impressionistic and vague notion of size.) Moreover, at this stage children reason that, although some transformations, such as the popping of popcorn and the rising of bread dough, produce something with altered gross volume (what Piaget and Inhelder call "global volume"), still, the sum of atomic volumes (what they call "corpuscular volume") will remain the same— unless, of course, something has been added or taken away.

There seems also to arise at Stage IV the idea of density as a relation between weight, objectively understood now, and volume, conceived now three-dimensionally. Even more impressive, there seems to develop at this stage the idea that the difference between the weights of bodies of the same volume can be understood as the difference between compactness or looseness of the atoms in those bodies, where the densities, and indeed the volumes, of the atoms themselves are thought to be standard.

To me, one of the most remarkable things about this story is that it comes close to recapitulating classical atomism—not modern atomic theory, of course, but the metaphysical system first elaborated by Democritus and Leucippus in the fifth century B.C. and presented, centuries later, by Lucretius in his *De rerum natura.* The thoughts expressed in the last paragraph, for example, seem to echo this passage from Lucretius:

Again, why do we find some things outweigh others of equal volume? If there is as much matter in a ball of wool as in one of lead, it is natural that it should weigh as heavily, since it is the function of matter to press everything downwards, while it is the function of space on the other hand to remain weightless. Accordingly, when one thing is not less bulky than another but obviously lighter, it plainly declares that there is more vacuum in it, while the heavier object proclaims that there is more matter in it and much less empty space.[2]

How is one to evaluate this great story of intellectual adventure that seems to repeat itself in the life of each normally developing child? For me it is a story of exciting intellectual achievement, a natural exercise in speculative metaphysics. Piaget sees things differently. Preoccupied, as he is, with the idea that cognitive development in children is a maturational process directed toward the mature competence of a standard adult, Piaget sees this conservation story as the stage-by-stage victory over intellectual deficits in the very small child. At the beginning of this developmental process, a child, on Piaget's understanding, is incompetent in various fundamental ways. Coming gradually to accept the principles of the conservation of substance, weight, and volume means, for Piaget, a gradual victory over that incompetence, an overcoming of certain, important cognitive deficits.

Piaget and Inhelder mention two cognitive deficits in particular that children overcome when they come to accept (CS), (CW), and (CV). They are egocentrism and phenomenalism. Thus, during Stage I, according to Piaget and Inhelder,

> both [matter and weight are] treated as functions of the direct perceptive relations imposed on the subject by his combined egocentrism and phenomenalism. [The child's] egocentrism reduces weight to a quality of what is being weighed or moved, and matter to a quality of what can be seen or retrieved by the eye . . . Phenomenalism, in its turn, prevents these children from recomposing and grouping the perceptive relations into rational systems and thus from going beyond the appearances. (45)

At Stage II, weight is said to be still "steeped in egocentrism and phenomenalism" (45), and the emergence of an objective conception of weight at Stage III is called a "new victory over egocentrism and phenomenalism" (46). They tell us that "the phenomenalist and egocentric approach to volume [however] persists at Stage III and . . . the dissociation [of the subjective from the objective] only appears at Stage IV" (63).

What are, in this context, egocentrism and phenomenalism? Unfortunately Piaget and Inhelder never give any clear account of what they mean by 'egocentrism' or 'phenomenalism.' Sometimes they suggest that egocentrism and phenomenalism together are the belief that "all things are what they appear to be on direct inspection" (75). There is here an echo of the great Greek Sophist, Protagoras, who is supposed to have said, "Man is the measure of all things, both of what is that it is, and of what is not, that it is not." Plato interpreted Protagoras to be saying that "each thing is to me as it appears to me, and is to you as it appears to you" (*Theaetetus* 152A). The idea is that there is no such thing as how the ball of clay is "in itself," whether, for example, it is in itself light, or heavy. If it seems heavy to me and light to you, that is the end of the matter.

Piaget's idea seems to be that children at the earlier stages are phenomenalists because they are wedded to the appearances (phenomena), that is, to how things seem. They are egocentric in that each child translates all questions about quantity into questions about how much there seems to be *"to me."*

Suppose Nicole, at Stage II, is asked, (1) Is the rolled-up ball of clay heavier than the clay was when it was a flattened sheet? To Nicole, at Stage II, that question can only mean, (2) Does the rolled-up ball *seem to you* heavier than the clay did when it was a flattened sheet? Let's suppose that the correct answer to (2) is "Heavier." If Nicole gives "Heavier" as her answer to (1), that will be, Piaget and Inhelder suggest, because her only way of understanding "Is the . . . ball heavier?" in (1) is: "Does the ball *seem* [phenomenalism] heavier *to you* [egocentrism]?"

Should we, too, understand this failure as the result of ego-centrism and phenomenalism in little Nicole? It seems strange to suppose that Nicole is firmly in the grip of phenomenalism. After all, having reached Stage II, she has, according to Piaget's own findings, already "constructed" the nonempirical, that is, non-phenomenal concept of substance. She insists that, quite regard-less of appearances, if no clay has been added and none taken away, there is still the same amount of the stuff, even though it now seems heavier than it seemed before.

Moreover, already at Stage IIA, according to Piaget, children are quick to suppose that there exist atoms too small to be seen. Thus, when a child at this stage is asked what happened to the dissolved sugar, the child answers, "It's in crumbs, in tiny little crumbs that nobody can see." Not even with a magnifying glass? the interrogator wants to know. "No," replies the child, "they're much too small" (83). Again, this hardly justifies a claim of child-hood phenomenalism.

As for egocentrism, extreme egocentrism would be a total failure to recognize that there even exist other subjects, or other points of view. Piaget's work on very young infants, who seem not yet to have the concept of a permanent object, has been thought to establish that infants are extremely egocentric. How-ever, even Piaget does not suppose that children in the age range we have been discussing (seven to twelve years old) are extremely egocentric. Nor do the experimental results he and Inhelder report support any such claim. What we might call "moderate ego-centrism" would be either (a) a lack of interest in how things look (feel, seem, etc.) to other subjects, or else (b) an inability to suc-ceed in imagining how things look (feel, seem, etc.) to other sub-jects or from other points of view.

Remarkably, there is no attention at all in these experiments to what children expect adults, or other children, to say in answer to the conservation questions. Does Nicole think that to her school chum, Jacques, the rolled-up clay will seem heavier than the flattened-out clay? Piaget and Inhelder don't ask the question.

They don't try to determine whether a child like Nicole is interested in how the clay feels to her friend.

Strangely, it is the "feelings" of the balance that Piaget and Inhelder attend to. "There can be no clearer demonstration of these children's egocentric approach to weight," they write; "weight is an unquantifiable quality that affects the scales in precisely the same way as it affects the human hand" (32). Their idea seems to be that these children are egocentric because they are poor at imagining how the clay will feel to the balance! Surely that is a very bad way of understanding what is going on.

It isn't really the case that Nicole begins by being bad at imagining how the clay will feel to the balance, and then gets better at taking the balance's feelings into account. Rather she learns to make a distinction between how things feel and how they really are, where the scales are supposed to help her determine, with respect to weight, how things really are.

I conclude that the claim that these conservation findings show children gradually overcoming egocentrism and phenomenalism is unsubstantiated.

Putting aside the specific claims of egocentrism and phenomenalism Piaget and Inhelder make, can one still say that children overcome important cognitive deficits as they pass through this development? Before we can answer that question, we need to ask what status (CS), (CW), and (CV) enjoy. Are they truths of reason—what philosophers call *a priori* truths? If not, are they fundamental laws of science? If they are neither of these, are they at least important empirical truths?

In fact, the principles cannot be *a priori* truths, fundamental truths of science, or even lower-level empirical truths. The reason is that they are not truths at all; they are all false.

As Piaget and Inhelder make clear throughout their discussion, what they call the conservation of substance is a principle of the conservation of *matter*. But as older children learn in their high school physics courses, it is not matter, but mass/energy, that is guaranteed to be conserved. So (CS) is false.

As for (CW), many, if not most, children these days know about "weightlessness" in space travel. They know, then, that (CW) doesn't hold in a space ship. And so, long before they take a physics class, they know that (CW), as a universal principle, is also false.

Similarly, (CV) is also defective. Not too long ago I read in the *New York Times* of an Iowa scientist who had created a sort of anti-rubber. If it is stretched in one direction, it expands in every other direction. The author of the *Times* article commented (without even mentioning Piaget): "At first glance, such materials seem to violate the law of Conservation of Volume. Actually, though, there is no such law—unlike energy, volume is not a quantity that needs to remain constant in a physical system."[3] Though (CS), (CW), and (CV) are all false, "constructing" them is, nevertheless, a considerable achievement. As I have already indicated, (CS) seems to me an especially satisfying principle. The fact that children do not, on their own, come up with the idea that mass can be transformed into energy should not obscure their achievement in constructing (CS). Piaget himself makes clear that (CS) is not arrived at on the basis of observations. As the experiments reveal, children accept (CS) long before they suppose that either weight (as revealed by the balance) or volume (as revealed by water level in the beaker) is conserved.

Somehow each child is led to think something like this: "No stuff has been added and no stuff taken away; so there must be the same amount of stuff left; it is just in a different shape now, with a different weight and volume." That is a wonderful exercise in rationalistic metaphysics. As it turns out, the world doesn't cooperate. The world allows for the transformation of matter into energy. But one couldn't know that, just by thinking about squashed clay balls or dissolved sugar cubes.

It isn't, then, that the cognitive development Piaget charts with

his conservation experiments records the wiping out of real cognitive deficits, whereas the philosophical thinking I prize is only
a kind of intellectual play. For one thing, the achievements Piaget
touts are not the acceptance of truths at all, but rather the "construction" of intellectually satisfying principles that all turn out to
be false. Even if it is essential to cognitive maturity that children
go through stages in which they come to accept, successively,
(CS), (CW), and (CV), this development cannot be viewed as a
step-by-step victory of truth over falsehood.

Secondly, aspects of the development Piaget charts are, in fact,
quite philosophical. In particular, the "construction" of (CS) with
its component principles—(i) nothing comes out of nothing, and
(ii) nothing passes away into nothing—is wonderfully philosophical. So, too, is the atomic theory that begins to emerge already
at Stage II. As Piaget himself notes, this theory is quite like the
ancient philosophical theories of Democritus and Leucippus. It is
much less like modern atomic theory, which, despite using the
term 'atom,' (meaning, originally, "indivisible thing") is not com-
mitted to supposing that there really are any "ultimate," indivisible
particles.

The children's atomic theory includes the idea that each atom
has a determinate volume. On that theory it at least makes sense
to suppose that, for example, the sum of the volumes of the atoms
in an exploded grain of popcorn is the same as the sum of the
atoms in the grain before it was popped. In modern atomic theory,
by contrast, the idea of the volume of an atom has no clear application.

The children's atomic theory is a wonderful intellectual construction. It is, in fact, a philosophical construction. We should
not denigrate its intellectual beauty just because, in the real world,
(CV) is false.

Thus the main difference between Piaget and me is this:
Whereas Piaget searches for an age-related sequence of cognitive
developments that are to be found in all normal children and that

form an age-related sequence, I am also interested in, say, Kristin's hypothesis that all the world is made of color, even though there is no age at which all, or even most, children can be expected to come up with that thought.

There is something more to add. I am myself still reflecting on why any of us might think that (CV) is true, not just children of a certain age. I would like to get clearer than I now am about what makes (CV) such a plausible principle, even though it turns out to be false.

In the seventeenth century there was an interesting debate on whether every body, no matter how small, is intrinsically elastic, or whether the very smallest bodies, the atoms, are rigid and impenetrable. If the atoms are rigid, then elasticity is a property of bodies that are compounds of atoms, for example, a rubber ball. It will be explained as the capacity of these larger bodies (for example, the rubber ball) to let their constituent atoms become more densely or more loosely packed.

This debate on whether elasticity is an intrinsic property of all bodies, including atoms, or only a derived property of bodies that are themselves composed of atoms, is crucial for (CV). Obviously if even atoms are themselves elastic, (CV) does not hold.

I find this debate fascinating. I want to understand better than I now do, what gives each side in the debate its plausibility. This kind of interest also marks me off from Piaget and Inhelder. If they were ever intrigued by a debate of this sort, they have carefully concealed their interest from the readers of their book.

5

Moral Development

Is it a good idea to think of moral development as concept displacement? That is, is it a good idea to conceive moral development as exchanging a less adequate concept of honesty, courage, justice, obligation, or whatever, for a better one, and then exchanging that concept for a still better one?

How would the story go? Well, consider the concept of moral obligation. One might say that a child starts out with only a very external concept of obligation. According to this "stage-one concept," an obligation is something someone *else* holds one responsible for, not a responsibility one lays on oneself. The relevant "somebody else" would be an authority figure—Mother, Father, Teacher, Priest, Police Officer. The embedded concept of being held responsible would also be external in that it would have to do with the threat of physical punishment and the promise of material reward.

Thus suppose Mother tells me not to raid the cookie jar. She goes off to the grocer's and leaves me alone in the house. I am obliged not to eat any cookies while she is away. If I am very small, perhaps my understanding of being held responsible for keeping my hands out of the cookie jar would be limited to the realization that, if I do take another cookie and Mother finds out, I will probably be spanked.

Getting a more advanced concept of obligation might then consist in getting a more nearly internal concept of being responsible for keeping my hand out of the cookie jar. The threat of physical punishment and the promise of material reward might come to play no essential role in my understanding of my obligation. Instead, the fear that Mother might show disappointment by the look on her face would, perhaps, be threat enough. At this point, though, my concept of obligation would still be somewhat external in that there would have to be someone outside me, some external authority figure, to hold me responsible for whatever it is I am obligated to do.

At a third stage of moral development, on this concept-displacement model, I might eventually learn to function as my own authority figure, my own "lawgiver." I could then recognize an obligation to respect the wishes of my mother, or the obligation to be brave, or to tell the truth, even when there was no likelihood that Mother or Father, Teacher or Priest, would be able to check up on me. To be sure, I might want the approval of some authority figure. I am only human. And if I lied or behaved in a cowardly fashion, I would doubtless prefer that no authority figure find out. But at the third stage I would find nothing odd or paradoxical in the suggestion that I have an obligation, say, not to read my office-mate's electronic mail, even though that responsibility has never been specifically laid on me by my parents or teachers, even my boss, and it is not backed by the promise of external reward or the threat of external punishment.

Is this a good way to think of moral development? One thing that should give us pause is the realization that, according to this model of moral development, those children who are at the first stage in the process are really only "pre-moral" beings. The reason they are only pre-moral is that their concept of obligation as the realization that they will likely be punished if they do such-and-such is not a concept of *moral* obligation at all.

To see that this is so, imagine that I live in a police state. I may agree to report to the police the daily activities of my neighbor;

I may agree to do this even though I consider such reporting distasteful, perhaps even wrong. I may do it anyway out of fear that I will otherwise lose my job. In any case, I can accept the obligation the police lay on me to spy on my neighbors without my thinking of it as being a moral obligation, and without its being for me a moral obligation.

If the concept of obligation that children have includes no recognition, on any level, of the moral appropriateness of at least some of the things they feel obligated to do, then their concept of obligation is not a concept of moral obligation at all. It is just the recognition that there are some things we get punished, or rewarded, for doing.

Some people may welcome this consequence of the concept-displacement model of moral development. They will agree that young children are, in fact, only pre-moral agents. For them the concept of obligation a child has at, say, age five has to do with morality only in the very minimal sense that one needs to have this concept so as to be able to exchange it later on for a concept with real, moral content. It is thus a genuinely pre-moral concept.

I, myself, consider this consequence enough by itself to discredit the concept-displacement approach to understanding moral development. It is not that I think young children are morally better than the concept-displacement approach allows. It is rather that I think young children, even very young children, are at least genuinely moral agents. By that I do not mean just that they are capable of sometimes doing the right thing. I mean that they are capable of sometimes doing the right thing for the right reason, or, at least, for a good reason, a genuinely moral reason. They may not be able to articulate well the reasons they have for fulfilling their obligations. But they are capable of recognizing and accepting a moral obligation as a claim on them that is something different from a threat of punishment or a promise of reward.

What I have in mind is something rather ordinary, but yet also profound. One can see it, I think, in this description of and commentary on the behavior of an infant, Michael, then only fifteen months old:

> [Michael] was struggling with his friend, Paul, over a toy. Paul started to cry. Michael appeared concerned and let go of the toy so that Paul would have it, but Paul kept crying. Michael paused, then gave his teddy bear to Paul, but the crying continued. Michael paused again, then ran to the next room, returned with Paul's security blanket, and offered it to Paul, who then stopped crying.

The psychologist Martin L. Hoffman, perhaps the leading researcher on empathy in young children, comments:

> First, it does seem clear that Michael assumed that his own teddy, which often comforts him, would also comfort his friend. Second, its failure to do this served as corrective feedback, which led Michael to consider alternatives. Third, in considering the processes underlying Michael's final, successful act, three possibilities stand out: (1) he was simply imitating an effective instrumental act observed in the past; that is, he had observed Paul being comforted with the blanket. This can be tentatively ruled out, since Michael's parents could not recall his ever having such an opportunity. (2) In trying to think of what to do, he remembered seeing another child being soothed by a blanket, and this reminded him of Paul's blanket—a more complex response than might first appear, since Paul's blanket was out of Michael's perceptual field at the time. (3) Michael, as young as he was, could somehow reason by analogy that Paul would be comforted by something that he loved in the same way that Michael loved his own teddy.[1]

Hoffman adds: "I favor the last interpretation, although it does postulate a complex response for a young child."

It is worth noting that the interpretation that Hoffman says he favors does not account for Michael's behavior unless we also assume that Michael somehow thought he *ought* to comfort Paul.

However exactly one interprets this particular incident, it seems to me obvious that *some* very young children *sometimes* act in genuinely moral ways, not just in pre-moral ways. That means, they act with some kind of understanding that what they are doing is a good thing to do because, say, it will help someone out, or comfort someone, and not just that it might be a way to avoid being punished or a way to get rewarded. Since the concept-displacement approach to moral development allows children at the earliest stages only a pre-moral understanding of what they are doing, it is for that reason defective.

Let's see how this point plays itself out within the terms of the most influential contemporary theory of moral development, that of Lawrence Kohlberg. Kohlberg presents subjects with moral dilemmas and then grades their responses, in particular, the *justifications* they offer for their solutions to the dilemmas, so as to locate each subject at one of six or so stages of moral development.[2] The most famous of Kohlberg's dilemmas is this one:

> In Europe, a woman was near death from a special kind of cancer. There was one drug that the doctors thought might save her. It was a form of radium that a druggist in the same town had recently discovered. The drug was expensive to make, but the druggist was charging ten times what the drug cost him to make. He paid $400 for the radium and charged $4,000 for a small dose of the drug. The sick woman's husband, Heinz, went to everyone he knew to borrow the money, but he could only get together about $2,000, which is half what it cost. He told the druggist that his wife was dying, and asked him to sell it cheaper or let him pay later. But the druggist said, "No, I discovered the drug and I'm going to make money from it." So Heinz got desperate and considered breaking into the man's store to steal the drug for his wife.[3]

As I say, subjects are assigned by Kohlberg to a stage of moral development, not according to what they say Heinz should do (for example, steal the drug), but rather according to the *justification* they offer for whatever they say that Heinz should do. (For example, the subject might say, "He should steal the drug and give it to his wife because saving somebody's life is more important than whether you steal.")

At Stage 1 a subject will exhibit what Kohlberg calls "the punishment and obedience orientation." At Stage 2 an elementary reciprocity emerges, but it amounts only to "You scratch my back and I'll scratch yours." Stages 1 and 2 constitute what Kohlberg calls the "Preconventional Level" of moral development.

Stages 3 and 4 make up the "Conventional Level." At Stage 3 one has achieved the "good-boy-nice-girl orientation"; Stage 4 is the "law and order" orientation.

Stages 5 and 6 constitute what Kohlberg calls the "Postconventional," "Autonomous," or "Principles" level. Stage 5 is based on the idea of a social contract. And, finally, at Stage 6 "right is defined by the decision of conscience in accord with self-chosen *ethical principles* appealing to logical comprehensiveness, universality and consistency."[4]

During some thirty years of investigation, Kohlberg and his collaborators amassed a staggering amount of evidence to show that the order of this development is fixed, in that no one reaches stage $n + 1$ without first going through stage n, and there is no regression to an earlier stage.[5]

Kohlberg's scheme seems to show little interesting cultural bias. (By 'interesting cultural bias' I mean bias that cannot be eliminated by the sensitive redescription of Kohlberg's dilemmas to fit other cultures.) As one recent investigator has put the matter,

> The evidence suggests that Kohlberg's interview is reasonably culture fair when the content is creatively adapted and the subject is interviewed in his or her native language. The invariant sequence proposition was also found to be well supported, because stage skipping and stage regressions were rare and always below the level that could be attributed to measurement error.[6]

For these and other reasons, Kohlberg's theory is one of the best articulated and most thoroughly supported theories in all developmental psychology. Nevertheless, many people are profoundly dissatisfied with it. Perhaps my comments about the inadequacy of the concept-displacement approach to understanding moral development reveal an important source of that dissatisfaction.

Does Kohlberg's theory make clear why the concept of obligation a child has at Stage 1 ("punishment and obedience orientation") or Stage 2 ("you scratch my back and I'll scratch yours") is a moral concept at all, even if only a primitive moral concept? The answer is no.

A Kohlbergian might reply by pointing out that the first two stages are characterized as the "pre-moral level." The idea is, presumably, that the concepts of obligation a child has at these stages are moral only in the sense that one has to develop each of them and move on to something else in order to arrive at a genuinely moral concept. Such a reply seems unsatisfactory for two reasons. First, it is surely implausible to suppose that not a single subject at Stages 1 or 2 has any understanding at all of what real morality consists in. Second, a similar difficulty recurs anyway at Stage 3, and perhaps even at Stage 4. One who conforms to expectations simply to avoid disapproval (Stage 3) or even one who acts to maintain the "given social order for its own sake" (Stage 4)[7] has not, it seems, *or at least not for those reasons*, attained a specifically moral understanding of obligation.

It begins to look as though all stages before Stage 5, or even Stage 6, are really pre-moral stages. Since, according to Kohlberg's research, hardly anyone, perhaps no one, reaches Stage 6, and only a small minority reach even Stage 5, we are driven to the unwelcome conclusion that the vast majority of people do not have a specifically moral concept of obligation. It is not just that most people do not usually act morally; that would hardly be a surprising conclusion. What is both surprising and objectionable is the conclusion that the vast majority of people do not have any real understanding of what morality consists in.

This worry is underlined by the fact that Kohlberg himself

defines morality in terms of impartiality, universalizability, reversibility, and prescriptivity. If Kohlberg is right and a judgment is moral if, and only if, it exhibits those formal features, then the concepts of obligation one has at lower stages of development are not even primitive moral concepts; they are not moral concepts at all.

This worry can be made concrete by appeal to a hypothetical example. Suppose Susan, age six, is given a Kohlberg interview and is found to be at Stage 1. What this means is that Susan's ability to reason her way through a moral *dilemma* and to resolve a moral *conflict*, and especially her ability to articulate such a resolution, are very primitive. Now suppose that when cookies and orange juice are distributed to Susan's class in school, Susan herself happens to get two cookies, whereas James, through a simple oversight, gets none, and everyone else gets one. We can imagine that Susan first rejoices in her good fortune, but then, noting that James got no cookie at all, gives one of hers to him. She has done the fair thing; she has done what she ought to do, what, in those circumstances, morality requires.

Of course Susan might have given James her extra cookie out of fear that she would be reprimanded for accepting two cookies when James had none. Or she might have given him a cookie in the hope of praise from her teacher, or a favor, later on, from James. She might have had these motivations. But there is no reason to suppose she *has* to act out of fear of punishment or hope of reward. In particular, and this is the crucial point, the fact that she scores at Stage 1 in a Kohlberg interview does not mean that she *cannot* act out of a sense of fairness when she is *not* confronted with a moral dilemma, let alone confronted with the need to resolve and justify her resolution of a moral dilemma.

A Kohlbergian might reply that Susan does not really have a sense of fairness if her moral *reasoning* is at Stage 1. She may be modeling behavior that she observes in others, or conforming to pressures from adults or peers, but she is not really acting from a sense of fairness unless she can give Stage 5 or Stage 6 *reasoning* to resolve a moral dilemma.

In my view, this Kohlbergian response focuses on only one of the several dimensions of moral development and ignores all the rest. To make this point clear, let me outline an alternative conception of moral development.

Each of us can bring to mind, for each major term of moral assessment in our active vocabulary (for example, 'moral,' 'immoral,' 'fair,' 'unfair,' 'honest,' 'lying,' 'brave,' 'cowardly,' and so on) at least one paradigmatic situation to which we think the term applies. Our understanding of what these terms mean includes our ability to assimilate other cases to these paradigms.

Our first paradigm of bravery is, perhaps, succeeding in not crying in the doctor's office when we are about to be stuck with a needle. For telling a lie my paradigm may be denying, falsely, that I ate little brother's piece of candy when he was out playing. For fairness, the paradigm may be dividing the cookies evenly among the members of a school class so that each one gets the same number of cookies.

It will be objected that I am making a naive mistake here of the kind that Socrates' hapless interlocutors are always making in the early Platonic dialogues. An example of lying, even a paradigm example, is not *what lying is*. Surely, the objection continues, only someone who can define 'lying' satisfactorily really knows what lying is, and only such a person has succeeded in latching onto the immoral behavior that is properly called "lying."

My reply is twofold. First, it is an open question whether any of us can give an entirely satisfactory definition of 'lying.' (We should not be surprised that the early Platonic dialogues end in perplexity!) Yet most of us have a working grasp of what lying is. Therefore, having a working grasp of what lying is, is something other than being able to give an entirely satisfactory definition of 'lying.' In fact, it can consist in having a basic understanding of central paradigms of lying and the ability to compare other cases to these paradigms so as to determine whether they, too, should count as cases of lying.

Second, Socrates' technique in the early Platonic dialogues requires his interlocutors (and his readers!) to test out suggested definitions with their own intuitions. Thus Socrates in Book I of the *Republic* rejects Cephalus's definition of 'justice' ('telling the truth and paying your debts') by asking, rhetorically, whether one should return a weapon to its owner if, in the meantime, the owner has gone mad. As readers, we are expected to answer, "No, of course not." But on what basis can we give that answer if we have, as yet, no satisfactory definition of 'justice'? Clearly such testing of suggested definitions by counterexample is a futile exercise unless we already have a working grasp of the relevant term of moral assessment. Having such a grasp may consist simply in having a basic understanding of central paradigms and the ability to assess other cases by reference to those paradigms.

In my view moral development takes place across at least five different dimensions. First, there is the dimension of *paradigms*. A fabrication to escape punishment is a good first paradigm for lying. A misrepresentation to gain some advantage for oneself may be a second paradigm. (Lisa says she doesn't know what time it is— though she does, really—so as to be allowed to watch the rest of her TV program.) A group conspiracy to flout authority may be a third paradigm. (Albert tells the teacher he did not see who shot the spitwad even though he saw Leonard do it.)

A second dimension of moral development is relative success in offering *defining characteristics*. 'Saying something naughty the way Louis did' may be a simple, but appropriate, beginning. 'Uttering a falsehood' will be an improvement. 'Uttering a falsehood when you know better' is still better. 'Saying something you know is false to deceive someone else' is even better than that.

It is important to recognize, however, that none of these definitions is entirely satisfactory. Consider the last one ('Saying something you know is false to deceive someone else'). Suppose the teacher wants to find out who spread mustard on the wash-basins in the school washroom. She already has circumstantial evidence that my school chum Ben did it. Moreover, she has good reason to think that I witnessed the awful deed. But she cannot punish Ben unless a witness comes forward. She asks me and I deny that Ben did it. The teacher may realize that I am protecting my friend. (I have often done that before.) There is no deception involved. I may even realize that the teacher realizes that I am protecting my friend. Still, when I say that I didn't see Ben spread mustard on the wash basins, I tell a lie.

So the last definition is also defective. Moreover, I do not know how to repair it. Perhaps someone can offer a definition of 'lying' that fits all our cherished intuitions and is also informative. But the important point is that no one *need* be able to do this to have a working grasp of what lying is. To begin with, one need only have a basic understanding of one central paradigm.

A third dimension of development concerns the *range of cases* that fall under each term of moral assessment and how we deal with borderline cases. Is writing a bad check, when one knows that one's balance is insufficient to cover the check, a case of lying? Can a photograph lie? Is it lying for a student who was thrown out of college to wear the college tie?

A fourth dimension of moral development concerns the *adjudication of conflicting moral claims*, or to put the matter less tendentiously, the adjudication of apparently conflicting moral claims. Sometimes telling a lie is not being naughty; sometimes it is one's duty. How can this be? Though it is *prima facie* wrong to tell a lie, other moral claims may override the demand to tell the truth. We develop morally as we get better and better at thinking our way through such conflicts, or apparent conflicts.

Fifth, there is the dimension of *moral imagination*. Michael, at fifteen months, seems to have had the imagination to understand Paul's distress and to think of getting Paul's security blanket so that Paul would be comforted. Even at that very young age, Michael was quite advanced along the dimension of moral imagination.

Of course Michael's experience of the world and his understanding of how it works will be very limited at fifteen months. A very young child will not be able to empathize with, say, a victim of racial or gender discrimination because the child's experience and understanding of society are too limited. In general, we may hope to advance along the scale of moral imagination as we grow older and our experience of life becomes broader and deeper.

Yet this need not happen. People become overwhelmed by the problems of the society around them, or increasingly preoccupied with their own personal agendas. When that happens, even a very young and inexperienced child can catch us adults up short with a direct, empathetic response to, say, a homeless person trying to keep warm in a cardboard box under a bridge. A child's naive question can awaken our sleeping imagination and sympathy, and even move us to take moral action.

On the view I advocate, then, moral development takes place across these five different dimensions. Kohlberg concentrates on only one, namely, the fourth dimension (adjudicating moral conflicts or dilemmas). But long before a child will have to deal with moral dilemmas, let alone give a justification for resolving a dilemma, the child can have a strong empathetic response to the victims of suffering, or injustice, and a working understanding of central paradigms for terms of moral assessment.

Most of us never lose the paradigms we first assimilated in childhood. The equal division of cookies remains for us a paradigm of distributive justice. As Susan grows and develops we hope she will enlarge her stock of paradigms from handing out cookies fairly to distributing work assignments fairly among workers of varied abilities, to, perhaps, refusing to change the rules in the middle of a game. And we hope Susan will grow along other dimensions of moral development as well. But the simple paradigms of distributive justice will stay with her permanently. And no contrast between the virtuosity of her later reasoning and the naiveté of her early appeal to simple paradigms can establish that those early actions were not really performed from a sense of fairness.

Parents sometimes report to me that one child in their family got recognized early on as the "justice person" in that family. Perhaps it all began with cookie distribution at age three. But it continued through middle childhood, late childhood, and adolescence. This particular child would always be the person in that family who would ask, "But is that really fair?" Mother or Father might be called on to reassess things in answer to a question like that from a child. And the "justice person" needn't be the oldest child of the family, either.

Theories of cognitive and moral development often encourage us to distance ourselves from children—both from the children around us and from our own childhood selves. Such distancing sometimes produces a new respect for children. After all, it warns us against faulting children for shortcomings that express, according to the theories, immature cognitive and moral structures that are entirely normal for children of the given age range.

Yet such distancing can also encourage condescension. If we suppose that children live in conceptual worlds that are structurally different from ours, but that will naturally evolve into ours, how can we fail to be condescending toward children as moral agents?

The condescension, though understandable, is unwarranted. One reason it is unwarranted is that, as we saw in the last chapter, later structures are not entirely unquestionable accomplishments; characteristically, they are problematic in ways that philosophers never tire of exposing. Thus it is an open question whether anyone at all can provide an entirely satisfactory theory of justice or, as I remarked earlier, even an entirely satisfactory definition of 'lying.'

Another reason such condescension is unwarranted is that children, in their simple directness, often bring us adults back to basics. Any developmental theory that rules out, on purely theoretical grounds, even the possibility that we adults may occasionally have something to learn, morally, from a child is, for that reason, defective; it is also morally offensive.

6

Children's Rights

Should children enjoy rights they are not now thought to have, for example, the right to vote, the right to refuse to attend school or the right to divorce their parents? Or has the children's rights movement already gone too far?

In the midst of the 1992 U.S. presidential campaign a juvenile court case in Florida that raised these questions received widespread newspaper and television coverage. The issue that caught the public attention was whether children should have a right to divorce their parents.

On July 9, 1992, a judge in a Florida state court had ruled that a twelve-year-old boy had legal standing to petition to terminate his parents' rights so that he could be legally adopted by his foster parents, George and Lizabeth Russ. Initially referred to, presumably for his own protection, as "Gregory K.," Gregory himself revealed that his family name was Kingsley. It seemed appropriate that, in seeking to have the right to take his mother to court, on his own behalf, Gregory should also waive the protection of anonymity usually accorded minors.

After Gregory had appeared on national TV, interviewed by Barbara Walters, he became something of a celebrity. Because the case came to public attention in the midst of an election campaign for the U.S. presidency, indeed one in which the Republicans tried to make "family values" a central campaign issue, politicians soon tried to use Gregory's petition for their own political purposes.

The relevance of the case of Gregory Kingsley to Bill Clinton's candidacy was, no doubt, enhanced by the fact that Clinton's wife, Hillary Rodham Clinton, had worked for the Children's Defense Fund and had written several significant articles on children's rights.[1] George Bush took the opportunity of the judge's ruling to warn voters against "advocates of the liberal agenda," who, according to Bush, "even encourage kids to hire lawyers and haul their parents into court."[2]

Gregory's father had signed papers consenting to the termination of his parental rights. So it was the rights of the mother to have custody of the child that were at stake. As we soon learned, Gregory had lived for only eight months of the previous eight years with this mother and she had told the authorities when she gave him up the last time, "You take him back."

Gregory won his case in the Florida court. He seems also to have won widespread support in the court of U.S. public opinion. To mark the start of his new life, Gregory changed his name. Upon being officially adopted by his new parents he was to be Shawn Russ.

The case of Gregory Kingsley does not stand alone. We can see in both the United States and Europe a gradual extension of the legal rights children are recognized to have. The question of their moral rights, though separate, is not entirely distinct either. As we saw during the civil rights movement of the 1960s, recognizing the moral rights of a certain group of people often motivates us to work to change their legal status as well; conversely, changing the legal status accorded some group of people often encourages us to change our moral attitudes toward them as well.

Children raise an issue for two ethical principles in particular, namely, the Autonomy Principle and the Paternalism Principle. According to the Autonomy Principle, rational individuals should be self-determining. According to the Paternalism Principle, the autonomy of an individual may be restricted if such restriction is in that individual's own interest.[3]

Two distinct, but related, questions arise when we seek to bring a child under the Autonomy Principle:

(1) Is the child sufficiently rational, or rational in the right way, to be able to be self-determining?

(2) Would it be in a child's own interest to restrict that child's ability to be self-determining?

Question 1 concerns the application of the Autonomy Principle considered by itself. Question 2 concerns how paternalism bears on autonomy. It asks whether, in some particular case, the Paternalism Principle should "trump" the Autonomy Principle.

Applied to Gregory Kingsley, the Autonomy Principle, unrestricted, would validate Gregory's right to sue his mother for the termination of her parental rights, so that he could be adopted by the parents of a big and loving family, where he felt at home. But was Gregory sufficiently rational, at eleven or twelve years of age, or rational in the required way, to be able to exercise a right of self-determination (Question 1)? Most television viewers who saw him in the Walters interview, or watched him in court on Cable Network News (CNN), seem to have decided that he was. This is the way the *New York Times* reported Gregory's court appearance:

> The dark-haired sixth grader took the stand for more than an hour, his shoulders just barely rising above the witness stand. Exhibiting a presence and sophistication unusual for a boy his age, Gregory explained how he had met his foster father during a visit to the youth center where he had been placed.
>
> Gregory said that for almost two years while he was in foster care his mother never visited, called or wrote to him. "I just thought she forgot about me," he said on the stand in an unemotional voice. Later he explained that after he was taken from foster care the first

time, his mother had promised him he would never have to go back again. He was placed in foster homes twice after that, and Gregory testified that that was what had changed his feelings about his mother.

"I just thought she didn't care any more," he said, staring straight ahead at his lawyer, Jerri A. Blair, and not turning to look at his natural mother 20 feet away. "I figured that if she breaks her promise she just doesn't care very much."[4]

The reporter's comment, "exhibiting a presence and sophistication unusual for a boy his age," is worth reflecting on for a moment. It may well be that Gregory was unusually mature and sophisticated for a boy of his age. One suspects that such confidence and self-assurance as Gregory displayed would be especially unusual among children without stable home lives. But what the reporter in this case fails to mention is that a child's court appearance like this—live on CNN!—is altogether without precedent. We are hardly in position to judge how unusual "for a boy his age" his court appearance was, there being no other examples of a court appearance quite like this one. As much as anything else, this case may have encouraged people to ask whether it was just prejudice and condescension that led us to be surprised at Gregory's poise and sophistication.

As for Question 2 above, hardly anyone who followed this court case could have doubted that it was in Gregory's own best interest to be adopted by the new family. Since that is certainly what Gregory himself wanted to happen, there is no reason to think that restricting his autonomy would somehow have served his own interests. So in this case, anyway, the outcome might be thought to be the same whether Gregory's autonomy takes precedence or, alternatively, paternalism wins out over autonomy.

The case of Gregory Kingsley came exactly a quarter of a century after *In re Gault* (1967), the famous U.S. Supreme Court case in which minors were, for the first time, recognized to have the constitutional rights of due process, for example, the right to a counsel and the right to be warned that anything they say might be used in evidence against them.

We can expect that children will slowly be given more and more autonomy within our legal system, and that they will be allowed to exercise that autonomy at a younger and younger age. Is that a good thing? The judgment in the philosophical literature on children's rights is somewhat mixed.

In 1974 John Holt wrote, "I propose that the rights, privileges, duties, responsibilities of adult citizens be made *available* to any young person, of whatever age, who wants to make use of them."[5] In a similar spirit Howard Cohen published, six years later, his classic defense of the liberationist position on children's rights, *Equal Rights for Children*. This is the core of Cohen's position:

> I am not saying that nobody should have a right unless everyone has it . . . What I am saying is that unless relevant differences can be demonstrated, it is not right to treat people differently; it is unjust. In my view the differences between adults and children, such as they are, have been way overstated by those who support the double standard. Children are presumed to be weak, passive, mindless, and unthinking; adults are presumed to be rational, highly motivated, and efficient. The picture is drawn too sharply, of course, and nobody pretends that there are not exceptions. The trouble, however, is that a decent account of equal rights for children cannot be based on the exceptions. If it is, we have only readjusted the double standard; we have not eliminated it.[6]

Other important voices in the call for recognizing children's rights have been Bob Franklin and Shulamith Firestone. Firestone, in her work, emphasizes the connection between women's liberation and children's liberation: "We must include the oppression of children in any program for feminist revolution or we will be subject to the same failing of which we have so often accused men: of not having gone deep enough in our analysis, of having missed an important substratum of oppression merely because it didn't directly concern us."[7]

Laurence D. Houlgate, in his *The Child and the State: A Normative Theory of Juvenile Rights,* tries to stake out a more moderate position by allowing utilitarian considerations to temper the requirements of justice.[8] Laura Purdy, in her recent book, *In Their Best Interest? The Case Against Equal Rights for Children,* takes an explicitly utilitarian position in rejecting children's liberation. Purdy summarizes her position this way:

> First, by severing the asymmetrical legal ties that now bind parents and children together, equal rights would weaken appropriate parental authority. Two critically important consequences could be expected to follow. One is that parents would be more reluctant to provide for their children the kind of early training that now appears to be necessary for responsible and moral behavior later. The other is that adolescents would be less likely to take their parents' guidance seriously. Both of these consequences could reasonably be expected to have detrimental effects not only on children's own well-being but on their ability to participate constructively in a good society . . .
>
> Second, equal rights would require abolition of compulsory schooling. While it is obvious that there is a good deal the matter with the schools at present, it doesn't follow that what is the matter could best be gotten rid of by undermining their authority in this way . . .
>
> Third, equal rights would propel many children into the workplace at an early age, where, without education, they would be prepared for only the most menial jobs. There they would be subject to the uncertainties of fluctuating demand and might survive only by exposing themselves to various hazards or underbidding other needy workers.[9]

We can expect this debate to go on. We can also expect, as I have already indicated, that both the number and the types of rights that children are recognized to have will continue to grow. Moreover, we can expect that the minimum age at which children are recognized to have a given right, such as the right to take a parent to court, will recede. This is certainly the current trend. Perhaps conservative critics of children's rights like Laura Purdy will slow the trend; but they will not, I think, stop it, let alone reverse it.

Can we, without trying to settle the debate between advocates of children's rights and their detractors, find philosophical reasons to welcome this trend? I think we can. It is to that reasoning that I now turn.

Purdy, in her rejection of children's liberation, predicts that enlarging the realm of rights accorded to children will tend to undermine the authority of parents and the school. The problem of how to understand authority, and especially the problem of how to understand *rational authority*, is almost as old as philosophy. Reflection on that problem, I suggest, may give us reason to applaud the gradual liberation of children in our society, whatever fears and anxieties come with thinking about the expansion of children's rights.

In a stable and cohesive society parents and teachers are recognized by children as authority figures. Sociologically speaking, parents and teachers exercise authority over children by virtue of the social positions they occupy. But are such authority-structures rationally justifiable? To ask this question in its general form is to raise the philosophical problem of rational authority.

The philosophical problem of rational authority was first raised by Plato in his dialogue *Euthyphro*. In that dialogue Socrates meets Euthyphro, who is going off to a court to charge his father with impiety. Socrates expresses surprise that Euthyphro would bring a charge against his own father in a court of law. The implication of Socrates' surprise is that children owe their fathers honor and respect in such a way that it is almost unthinkable that they would charge their own fathers with a crime.

Euthyphro himself is unmoved by the suggestion that it might be impious of him to charge his father with impiety. He adds that the charge he wants to bring against his father is an extremely serious one; in fact, the charge is negligent homicide. The victim of this crime, as Euthyphro tells the story, had himself, in a drunken rage, killed one of the household slaves. Euthyphro's father had then bound this man hand and foot and had gone off to ask a priest what to do. Bound and abandoned in a ditch, the man had died from hunger and cold. Euthyphro holds his father responsible for this man's death and proposes to have his father indicted in court.

Thinking of negligent homicide as a form of impiety may first strike us as strange. But we should remember that "Do not kill!" is also one of the Ten Commandments in our Jewish and Christian traditions and that civil religion also plays at least an implicit role in our modern, secular government.

Socrates responds to Euthyphro's story in a manner that is typical for the figure of Socrates in Plato's early dialogues: he asks Euthyphro what piety is. The question seems appropriate, since Euthyphro, if he is charging his father with impiety, ought really to know what piety is. Much of the dialogue is taken up with Euthyphro's unsuccessful attempts to define 'piety' and 'impiety.'

The crucial point in the dialogue comes when, after Euthyphro has tried saying that piety is whatever all the gods love, Socrates asks his famous and profound question: "Is the pious loved by the gods because it is pious, or is it pious because they love it?" (*Euthyphro* 10A).

The "Euthyphro problem," as we may call it, can be translated into monotheistic terms more familiar to those of us in the Jewish, Christian, and Muslim traditions. Think of a religious believer who supposes that morality rests on divine command. For such a person, what it means to say "X is right" might be "God commands us to do X." And what it means, for such a person, to say "Y is wrong" is "God commands us not to do Y." Now come the Socratic questions, 'Is doing X right because God commands us to do X, or does God command us to do X because it is right?' and 'Is doing

Y wrong because God commands us not to do Y, or does God command us not to do Y because it is wrong?'

Consider murder and consider the claim 'Murder is wrong.' What that claim means, on the proposed analysis, is 'God commands us not to murder.' But is murder wrong because God commands us not to murder, or does God command us not to murder because it is wrong? If we choose the first alternative (murder is wrong because God commands us not to murder), we are *theological voluntarists*. From this point of view the volition or will, or command, or approval, of God is the bottom line. There is no accounting for God's will or command or approval on this alternative. On the other hand, if we choose the second alternative (God commands us not to murder because it is wrong to murder), we are *theological rationalists*. From this point of view there is, at least in principle, a way of accounting for God's will and God's commands. (God wills and commands what is right, and only what is right.) But that also means there is a moral standard independent of God, a moral standard by which God can be judged.

Theological voluntarism encourages the idea that, even if God's will and command were arbitrary, they would still determine what is right and wrong. Theological rationalism, by contrast, suggests that God is not all-powerful, since God must conform to the standards of morality.

The Euthyphro Problem also has a purely secular application, and that is, of course, why I am discussing it here. Suppose we say to the child, "What Mama says goes," that is, "What Mama says is right." Now the Euthyphro question is, 'Is it right because Mama says it, or does Mama say it because it is right?' If we take the first alternative, Mama's commands establish what is right, even when they are based on Mama's prejudice or whim. If we take the second, the fact that Mama says to do this, or that, drops out as inessential in understanding what makes something right. To know what makes something right we should look rather to the reasons Mama has for commanding the things she commands. On this view, in fact, Mama is accountable for what she commands, whereas on the previous one what Mama commands is automatically right.

Whatever we want to say about the original, theological version of the Euthyphro Problem, we should respond to the secular version by going between the horns of the dilemma. Suppose Mama says, "No more TV and no more Nintendo until you have finished your schoolwork!" This command has some *prima facie* claim to acceptance simply because Mama says it and Mama is in the position of authority with respect to the child. But, in a reasonable family, there will be some possibility for challenging the command—if not right away, then a little later perhaps, or on some occasion when such matters get discussed. The possibility of challenge, sometime, somewhere, means that command is only *prima facie* right because Mama commands it. On a deeper level, we must think that Mama commands it because it is right, or good, or advisable. If the challenge reveals that the command is not really warranted (say, because the child's homework is not due for another day, or because Mama had promised the child an hour of TV, or whatever), then the *prima facie* claim to rightness is overridden. It is the possibility of review that makes the authority rational, rather than merely arbitrary.

Purdy says that children's liberation will tend to undermine the authority of parents and teachers. But how is that authority to be understood? Let's concentrate, as before, on parental authority. If one has authority over a child simply by virtue of standing in a certain biological relationship to the child (by virtue of having borne or sired the child), then there needs to be, as indeed there is in our society, a legal mechanism for challenging that authority and calling it to account. As things now stand, and have stood for a long time, there are ways for some person or agency to go to court to challenge the assumed authority of a negligent or abusive parent over a child. The new question is whether children themselves should have "standing" in court to petition the court on their own behalf.

Let's go back to the case of Gregory Kingsley. As TV reports on the evening news made quite clear, Gregory's mother had long ago given up her responsibility for him; she had abandoned him to state agencies. Even if she did now want him back, she was not in position to provide him with a satisfactory home. (In fact, evidence that she herself was battered by her current lover suggested that she was not even able to provide herself with a satisfactory home.)

Of course, the judge in Florida could have terminated the mother's parental rights to Gregory without recognizing Gregory's right to petition the court on his own behalf. So the issue is not whether a biological parent's rights to her child are absolute, or whether they may be terminated against her will when the court deems such termination to be in the child's best interest. The issue is whether the child, in this case, twelve-year-old Gregory, should be recognized to have a right to petition the court on his own behalf and have the court respond to *him*, rather than just to his interests. Put in terms of the philosophical problem of rational authority, the issue is whether the court should recognize Gregory as a rational agent, able to make up his own mind on this matter, to whom the court is beholden to justify its exercise of authority in reviewing his mother's authority over him. The interviews with Gregory in the media and Gregory's court appearance give us good reason to say "Yes, Gregory is mature and reasonable enough for the court to deal with him directly as a directly interested party in the dispute."

Some politicians have discussed the idea of children having a right to divorce their parents as if, having such a right, they could simply walk out on their parents with impunity. As we can see from the case of Gregory Kingsley, however, having such a right might simply give children standing in a court of law to make certain petitions on their own behalf and have the court respond to *them* (as well as to their parents, of course) rather than simply to a court-appointed or court-recognized guardian.

In an ideal family, children, as they grow older, become more and more free to ask for a review of rules, practices, and decisions that regulate their lives within the family. That gradually increasing right to ask for review recognizes several important truths: (1) as they grow up, children are increasingly able to function as agents on their own behalf; (2) allowing children gradually to make more and more decisions about their own lives contributes to developing the maturity they need to function well as adults; (3) recognizing a right to appeal parental decisions and review family practices that a child wishes not to accept carries with it the implicit understanding that these decisions and practices are not acceptable simply because a parent lays them down as "law"; rather, in the paradigm case, anyway, they are laid down because the parent considers them wise or correct.

The society's treatment of parental authority should parallel the way in which parents in an ideal family treat their own authority over children. Not only should Gregory Kingsley, if he is sufficiently mature, have a right to petition the court on his own behalf to have his mother's authority over him terminated; he should also have a right to have the court address its decision to *him*, not just address some guardian or agency assumed to represent him and his interests. This right of petition is what gives content to the idea that parental authority is not based solely on the accident of biological relation, but also on the testable claim that Gregory's parent is carrying out her responsibility to do what is right for him. Gregory's right to petition on his own behalf, and not simply through some third party, carries with it the recognition that, already at age twelve, Gregory is able to make reasonable judgments about whether his mother has been carrying out her responsibilities toward him; should the court deny his petition, he deserves to have the court explain to *him*, and not just to a guardian, that he is wrong, and why.

So should children be recognized to have rights they do not now enjoy, or to have them at a younger age than they now enjoy them? I think so, though I have not tried to present a full case for that conclusion in this chapter. What I have tried to do instead is much more limited. I have pointed out that our society is moving slowly in the direction of assigning more rights to children and assigning rights at an earlier and earlier age. And I have suggested that there is a way of understanding this development that makes it philosophically welcome. It is to see authorities in our society as *rational* authorities, people who, even if they first come to occupy their positions of authority by biological accident, can be appropriately called upon to justify their exercise of authority, and justify it in the presence of their children, as soon as those children are capable of making reasonable judgments about their own interests.

7

Childhood Amnesia

As a seven-year-old child I asked myself how I knew that my memory could be trusted. What concerned me was not whether events had really happened the way I thought I remembered them, for example, whether my memory of my last birthday, or my first day in school, was accurate. Rather what interested me was the possibility that huge chunks of my experience might simply have dropped out of my memory without my realizing it. If my memory were full of gaps, its very "gappiness" might disguise the gaps. How could I know?

To reassure myself, I devised a simple experiment. I would deliberately select very ordinary events, otherwise quite unworthy of recall, and assign each a number. Then, at a later time, I would attempt to recall event #1, event #2, and so on. I realized that I might later forget the whole experiment. In that way, a gap in my memory might wipe out the test for gaps in my memory. However, if I were able to remember the test later on, and if I were able to recall, or even *seem* to recall, otherwise quite uninteresting events to go with the numbers '1,' '2,' and so on, I would have, I thought, at least some minimal evidence that much of my waking life was indeed safely bound into my book of personal memory.

I did not know then that, according to John Locke, to be the same person as that seven-year-old child, brushing his teeth with the mixture of salt and soda Mother had thought best, in the bathroom of that little house on Camden Street, I would have to be able to "repeat the idea of [that] past action with the same consciousness [I have] of any present action . . ."[1] But I seem to have had the idea that whether I really was a persisting subject of such day-to-day experiences was somehow or other at stake in my amateurish experiment.

For some months after devising my experiment I would occupy moments of reflection with the attempt to recall once more those arbitrarily numbered events. I was pleased at the minimal reassurance I got this way of my continuing existence as a person.

I was also interested in the question of how far back into the past my memory went. What was my first memory? Sometime during my elementary school years I decided that the earliest experience I could remember was that of going down an enclosed slide at the Chicago World's Fair in 1933, when I was almost four. The event had been marked with special significance by my mother, who, as often happened in my childhood, had apparently thought me competent to look after myself and only later, when I didn't turn up as soon as she expected at the bottom of the slide, felt guilty that she had not given me closer supervision.

Though my memory of that event was, perhaps, solidified by my hearing the story told in the family, I retained confidence, a remnant of which I still have, that I actually remembered going down that slide in Chicago. The attendant had warned me to keep my hands at my side, which I dutifully did. But one result of pressing my hands to my side was that I lost my balance on the descent and got turned around and slowed down, until I hit my head on the pavement at the bottom. Apparently the blow was severe enough to make the event more memorable, but not severe enough to obliterate it.

Why do we care what our first memory is? Perhaps we care for somewhat the same Lockean reason that I concocted my memory experiment. Locke thought that being the same *human being*[2] as, say, the little baby shown in the faded photograph on my dresser top was very different from being the same *person* as that infant.

Being the same human being, according to Locke, consists in having a body that is simply a later stage of the body that baby has in the picture. But to be the same person requires, he thought, having a connecting memory—a memory of being held in my mother's arms on the occasion portrayed in the picture.

Suppose that, in fact, the body of that baby has, over the years, gradually turned into the body I now have. Then I am the same human being as that baby. But, having no memory of being held as a baby by my mother on any such occasion as that portrayed in the photograph, I could not be the same *person* as that infant in the picture. "It is plain," Locke wrote, "consciousness, as far as ever it can be extended, should it be to ages past, unites existences and actions, very remote in time, into the same person, as well as it does the existences and actions of the immediately preceding moment: so that whatever has the consciousness of present and past actions, is the same person to whom they both belong."[3]

So, on Locke's criterion of personal identity, even if I am the same human being as that baby in the faded photograph, I am not the same person. In fact, as a person, or at least as the person I now am, I came into being at the time I went down the enclosed slide at the Chicago World's Fair.

Looking at one's family photo album, or perhaps at family movies of one's early childhood, it is, in fact, quite easy to get the idea that the young child in those pictures is "not really me." And the reason for this sense of alienation from the child pictured there is the Lockean reason that one simply cannot remember doing or experiencing the things that child is pictured as doing or experiencing. One simply cannot remember *being* that child.

Sigmund Freud seems to have been the first investigator of childhood to call special attention to the phenomenon of childhood amnesia ("infantile amnesia"). This passage from Freud's "Three Essays on Sexuality" is characteristic:

What I have in mind is the peculiar amnesia which, in the case of most people, though by no means all, hides the earliest beginnings

of their childhood up to their sixth or eighth year. Hitherto it has
not occurred to us to feel any astonishment at the fact of this
amnesia, though we might have had good grounds for doing so.
For we learn from other people that during these years, of which
at a later date we retain nothing in our memory but a few unintel-
ligible and fragmentary recollections, we reacted in a lively manner
to impressions, and that we were capable of expressing pain and
joy in a human fashion, that we gave evidence of love, jealousy and
other passionate feelings by which we were strongly moved at the
time, and even that we gave utterance to remarks which were
regarded by adults as good evidence of our possessing insight and
the beginnings of a capacity for judgement. And of this we, when
we are grown up, have no knowledge of our own![4]

Freud goes on in this passage to link childhood amnesia with
hysterical amnesia and to suggest a psychological explanation for
both. "Can it be, after all," he asks, "that infantile amnesia, too, is
to be brought into relation with the sexual impulses of childhood?"
His answer is, of course, yes.

Freud claimed that psychoanalysis could unearth childhood
memories that are now inaccessible to us: "In psycho-analytic
treatments we are invariably faced by the task of filling up these
gaps in the memory of childhood; and in so far as the treatment
is to any extent successful—that is to say, extremely frequently—
we also succeed in bringing to light the content of these forgotten
years of childhood."[5]

Exactly how successful psychoanalysis is in unearthing childhood memories is a matter of some controversy. But presumably
the success it could be expected to have would concern memories
with sexual significance—typically, memories that involve in
some way a sexual attraction to one's parent. For this reason alone,
even a lifetime of psychoanalysis could be expected to uncover
only a small fraction of one's waking life as an infant or a very
young child.

Of course, when we stop to think about it, we realize that we can recall only a small fraction of our lives anyway—even our adult lives, even what we did last month or last week. With prodding I might be brought to remember my third- or fourth-grade teacher, and perhaps an incident or two from those school years. But there is no way I could be brought to remember what happened every day, let alone every waking hour and every waking minute of every day. So even if there are memories to connect me with every *year* of my life since, say, the age of six, most of the experiences of my waking life are forever lost from memory.

That simple fact is a good introduction to the most famous criticism of John Locke's memory criterion of personal identity. About a century after Locke published his memory criterion, the Scottish philosopher Thomas Reid subjected it to a devastating criticism.[6] Suppose, Reid said, a brave young officer, decorated for his heroism, had been beaten as a boy for robbing an orchard. And suppose further that, as an old general, this man could remember being decorated as a brave young officer, and that the young officer could remember being flogged as a boy, but the old general could no longer remember being flogged as a boy. Then we can use Locke's criterion to generate a contradictory conclusion. The old general both is and is not the same person as the young boy who got flogged for robbing the orchard. He is the same person because the old general, remembering being decorated, is the same person as the young decorated officer, and the young officer, remembering being flogged, is the same person as the orchard robber, and if $a = b$ and $b = c$, then $a = c$. Yet the old general is not the same person as the boy who was flogged for robbing the orchard, since the old general cannot remember this episode from his youth.

Any criterion that produces contradictory results is, for that reason, unsatisfactory. So Reid urged, correctly I think, that Locke's criterion of personal identity is unsatisfactory.

To deal with Reid's objection several philosophers have recently proposed a *neo*-Lockean account of personal identity.[7]

According to neo-Locke, the old general would not need to be able to remember being flogged as a child to be the same person as the child who got flogged. It would be enough that there be a chain of memory in the way Reid described. If the old general remembers being decorated as a young officer and the young officer remembers being flogged as a boy, this new "linking criterion" (as we may call it) would generate the conclusion that the old general is the same person as the young boy who was flogged.

In fact, the "linking criterion" allows for, not just a single intermediate link with a past episode, but as many intermediate links as you like. Thus, if I can remember going down the slide at the Chicago World's Fair in 1933 and hitting my head on the bottom, and the child who went down the slide at the fair in 1933 and hit his head on the bottom could remember getting a scooter for Christmas six months earlier, and the child who got the scooter could remember going shopping for red Wellington boots six months before that, then, by the linking criterion, I am also the child who went shopping for red "Wellies" a whole year before the earliest memory I can now call up.

What this new linking criterion of personal identity does is to include in the life of me, as a person, much that I can now no longer recall, in fact, *much, much* more than I can now recall. I am the person who did A if either I can now remember doing A, or else I can remember doing B and that person who did B can remember doing A, or I can remember doing C and that person who did C can remember doing B and the person who did B can remember doing A, and so on for as many intermediate memory links as you like.

Recent work on memory in infants suggests that, if we use a linking criterion of this sort for personal identity, the early childhood and even infancy that would certainly be lost to us on a standard Lockean criterion of personal identity will be ours after all. One experiment has shown that a memorable experience of an infant of only six months may be accessible to that child as

much as two years later.[8] So the capacity for episodic memory
extends back into very early infancy. But eventually, as we grow
up, almost all those very early episodic memories are apparently
lost.

What begins to develop in the three-year-old is so-called auto-
biographical memory.[9] By this time we can give our personal
memories at least a minimal "story line." Episodic memories that
seem irrelevant to the story we are able to tell about our lives
simply drop out.

For an adult, then, much of childhood is lost to direct recall.
Perhaps it never made it into the "long-term-memory bank"
anyway, or perhaps it got there but was later dislodged by the
development of autobiographical memory. But recognition of this
fact shouldn't make me think of my childhood self as an alien
creature, any more than I should think of the man who went into
the bank on, say, the third of October three years ago to withdraw
seventy-five dollars from my checking account as an alien creature.
(He was me!) I cannot now remember being the man who with-
drew the seventy-five dollars from my account on that occasion,
but the next week I still remembered withdrawing the money
when I sought to rationalize my bankbook. And the week after
that I remembered rationalizing my bankbook when I ordered new
check fillers, and so on, in an intertwined set of memory links that
connect the first experience with my present life, experience, and
memory.

And so it is, too, with my childhood. I can't now remember my
second day of school. But a week later I still could, when a friend's
mother asked me about the first week of school. And a week after
that I could remember being asked about the first week of school,
even though already the direct memory of the second day was
fading. Still, there are memory links that connect up that distant
day with the present one.

To find what I have just been saying satisfactory does not rule
out supposing that there are psychologically interesting gaps in

one's memory, including psychologically interesting gaps in one's memory of one's own childhood. Perhaps a Freudian or other account of amnesia might help us understand why some of these gaps are there. But it isn't that our childhoods are, in general, unrelated to us through memory. And so we do not have this reason for feeling, as a general thing, alienated from our childhood. The memory link that connects us with our very early selves may be convoluted; but then so are the links that connect us with the day-to-day existence we enjoyed last year, or last month, or even yesterday.

8

Childhood and Death

Many adults are shocked to realize that two classics of modern children's literature deal directly with death. They are shocked because the very idea of discussing death with children strikes them as offensively inappropriate. Yet not only are *Charlotte's Web* by E. B. White and *Tuck Everlasting* by Natalie Babbitt good books that children really like, they are also serious attempts to come to terms with our common mortality.[1]

Tuck Everlasting is a philosophical adventure story. Full of action and surprise, it is held together by a remarkably sustained, eloquent, and engrossing effort to convince Winnie, the young heroine, that the ordinary life of childhood, adulthood, old age, and death is vastly preferable to an everlasting life arrested at ten or seventeen or forty-two.

Winnie Foster, ten years old, who is about to drink from a spring in her family's wood, is suddenly kidnapped by Mae Tuck and her two sons. The Tucks eventually explain to Winnie that they all—father, mother, and two sons—drank from that spring eighty-seven years ago. The result is that they all stopped aging. "If you'd had a drink of it today," Mae tells Winnie, "you'd stay a little girl forever. You'd never grow up, not ever."

The Tucks point out that they don't fit into the society around them. They can't even stay in one place for long. "People get to wondering," as Mae puts it.

More basically, the Tucks simply don't fit into the world. Out in a rowboat on a summer's evening, Mae's husband, Tuck, tries to explain. "Everything's a wheel," he says, "turning and turning, never stopping. The frogs is part of it, and the bugs, and the fish, and the wood thrush, too. And people. But never the same ones. Always coming in new, always growing and changing, and always moving on. That's the way it's supposed to be. That's the way it is" (56). When their rowboat gets stuck, Tuck makes ready use of the analogy:

> But this rowboat now, it's stuck. If we didn't move it out ourself, it would stay here forever, trying to get loose, but stuck. That's what we Tucks are, Winnie. Stuck so's we can't move on. We ain't part of the wheel no more. Dropped off, Winnie. Left behind. And everywhere around us, things is moving and growing and changing. (56)

At one point Winnie blurts out, "I don't want to die." Tuck replies:

> Not now, your time's not now. But dying's part of the wheel, right there next to being born. You can't pick out the pieces you like and leave the rest. Being part of the whole thing, that's the blessing. But it's passing us by, us Tucks. Living's heavy work, but off to one side, the way *we* are, it's useless, too. It don't make sense. If I knowed how to climb back on the wheel, I'd do it in a minute. You can't have living without dying. So you can't call it living, what we got. We just *are*, we just *be*, like rocks beside the road. (57)

Tuck Everlasting gradually nudges its readers, whether children or adults, to the conclusion that any life that includes real living has a beginning, a middle, and an end. Given the choice between an unendingly arrested childhood and a life of the normal sort, the heroine of the story finally chooses mortality. The reader, whether nine or eighty-nine, is likely to approve the choice, or, if not actually approve it, at least understand it.

Schoolteachers and librarians report that this book is well liked by children. No doubt many adults, especially those who have not been able to confront their own mortality, recoil at the suggestion that a book for children should confront this topic, or that they can profit from reading it. They are wrong. In fact, I once heard a school librarian testify to the worth of having parents discuss this book, with their children, in a public setting. The librarian had run a "great books for children" group in which *Tuck Everlasting* was included. The children, who had been remarkably open and reflective in discussing the book among themselves, were especially interested to hear how their own parents responded to the book. The didn't know what their parents had to say about death, since the topic had never been broached at home. In the end, the parents seemed grateful to have been prodded into disclosing to their children their own fears and anxieties, particularly in response to such a wise story.

The popularity of *Charlotte's Web* is, in a way, even more surprising than that of *Tuck Everlasting*. It is, after all, a book in which there are passages like this one:

> The thought of death came to him and he began to tremble.
> "Charlotte?" he said, softly.
> "Yes, Wilbur?"
> "I don't want to die."
> "Of course you don't," said Charlotte in a comforting voice. (62)

To be sure, Wilbur is only a pig. And Charlotte is just a spider. Still, anyone who has come this far in the story will doubtless have come to identify with these characters, much as if they were human beings. No doubt the barnyard setting and the fact that the characters are not just animals, but talking animals, distance us somewhat from the theme of mortality, or at least mortality in "the real world." It is, after all, a talking pig's mortality and a talking spider's mortality that the story is about.

Nevertheless, the characters, though somewhat removed from "real life," are hardly remote. The engaging directness with which they talk about their situation makes the analogies to human life and death unmistakable.

By the time we are grown up, most of us have ourselves given something very much like Wilbur's speech, or had it given to us by someone else. I can remember during my graduate school days having my friend, Klaus, who was an exchange student from Berlin, tell of being awakened during the night by Shanti, an Indian graduate student in mathematics we both knew.

"What is it?" asked Klaus, who was struggling to wake up.

"I don't want to die," said Shanti.

Klaus, who had been a medical orderly in World War II with the German army on the Russian front, and who had made vivid comparisons in my hearing of his own war experience with Tolstoy's account of Prince Andre's battlefront experience in *War and Peace,* had himself had Shanti's thought many times.

"Of course you don't," he said to Shanti.

In *Charlotte's Web,* Charlotte does more than comfort her friend Wilbur; she saves him from slaughter by making him a famous pig. She does that by writing messages in her webs that celebrate Wilbur. E. B. White makes it clear to the readers of this story that writers do sometimes have the ability to make characters outlive their creator's lives.

The poignancy of the story arises from the touching irony that, as Charlotte realizes from the first, she herself is doomed to die at the end of the summer. Her last efforts, as her strength fades, produce an enormous egg sack, which is her only hope of a sort of afterlife.

Charlotte's Web is popular with children who have no experience with life-threatening illness or death. But it enjoys a special place in the lives of may children battling terminal illness, as Myra Bluebond-Langner reports in her pioneering work on leukemic children, *The Private Worlds of Dying Children:*

> The most popular book among these children was *Charlotte's Web.* When Mary and Jeffrey reached stage 5 [the stage of full awareness

of their illness], it was the only book they would read. Several
children at stage 5 asked for chapters of it to be read to them when
they were dying. But as one parent stated, "They never chose the
happy chapters." They always chose the chapter in which Charlotte
dies. After any child [in the pediatric oncology ward] died, the
book had a resurgence of popularity among the others.[2]

In a recent collection of papers, *Children and Health Care: Moral and
Social Issues*, two philosophers, Rosalind Ekman Ladd and Loretta
M. Kopelman, explore the reasons why this book might be so
popular among children dying of leukemia, and what message
they might get from it.[3] According to Ladd, "the main value statement that the book as a whole makes is this: What is natural is
good and dying which is natural and in accordance with nature is
a good dying and to be accepted, but a death which is unnatural
is a bad death and to be protested" (109). In those terms the initial
threat to kill Wilbur, because he was the runt pig, as well as the
somewhat later threat to slaughter him for meat, are both bad,
and to be resisted. But Charlotte's dying at the end of a spider's
normal life span is good, and something to be accepted.

Ladd tries to bring out some of the ways in which Charlotte's
death is a good one:

> She is aware of what is happening to her, she plans for it, lays her
> eggs, talks with her friends about it and says her good-byes. Much
> of the peacefulness that surrounds her death may be attributed to
> her foreknowledge and planning. Although the life-span of a spider
> cannot be changed, Charlotte is still able to exercise choice over
> some aspects of her dying. Her first great choice is to go with
> Wilbur to the Fair, even though that means she will die there
> instead of at home. Then she chooses to use her last days spinning
> words into her web to help Wilbur. (115)

As Ladd points out, families and medical personnel may help
dying children exercise choices that will make their deaths
approximate more closely to Charlotte's model of "the good

death." Yet, of course, a dying child, or even a child with a life-threatening illness, will learn in many different ways that there is nothing at all natural about the death of a child.

Loretta Kopelman, in her reply to Ladd, treats *Charlotte's Web* as, among other things, a response to the problem of evil. ("If the Creator is good, omniscient, and powerful, why do the innocent suffer pain and early death?", 126) She compares the response of White's story to Plato's response:

> Plato and White seem to picture suffering and evil in the world differently. For Plato, the non-moral evils of pain, untimely death, and loss cannot be eliminated from the world because they are part of what is. There is no way to make the chaotic world entirely fit real notions of goodness and justice. No one is to blame; this is a necessary feature of finitude. But the picture suggested in E. B. White's *Charlotte's Web* is that the world is not only as good as it can be (a view with which Plato might agree) but that when viewed from the right perspective, evil has a purpose or disappears as illusory. Life is a triumph, miracle, and glory. (126–127)

To back up her interpretation Kopelman quotes the penultimate paragraph to the story:

> Mr. Zuckerman took fine care of Wilbur all the rest of his days, and the pig was often visited by friends and admirers, for nobody ever forgot the year of his triumph and the miracle of [Charlotte's] web. Life in the barn was very good—night and day, winter and summer, spring and fall, dull days and bright days. It was the best place to be, thought Wilbur, this warm delicious cellar, with the garrulous geese, the changing seasons, the heat of the sun, the passage of swallows, the nearness of rats, the sameness of sheep, the love of spiders, the smell of manure, and the glory of everything. (White, 183)

Kopelman goes on to compare the two responses to the special evil of dying children:

Plato suggests nature is "contaminated," and pain and suffering simply are part of the conditions of finitude. The child who gets sick and suffers is "dealt a bad hand" by nature. White suggests another view, however, which may explain why children facing death find *Charlotte's Web* comforting. In this story, fears are expressed but we are reassured: everything is as good as it can be, evil and suffering are explained as necessary, death is not painful, and those who do not have to die (Wilbur) are saved. One is not abandoned since one is "never without friends." The dying person [Charlotte] is central, good, and wise. She is always loved and remembered as a good friend and a person of accomplishment. There is rebirth and continuity: "each spring there were new baby spiders." (127)

I suspect that not many parents or medical professionals discuss the problem of evil with seriously ill children. It's good then that they can read, in story form, at least one important response to it.

There will doubtless be those who protest that all this discussion rests on a sentimentalized over-interpretation of the capacities and responses of young children. Developmental psychologists have shown, these protesters will insist, that young children have no adequate concept of death. Therefore, young children with life-threatening illness cannot understand the threat they face, and so are incapable of discussing it as a manifestation of the problem of evil.

Susan Carey, in her *Conceptual Change in Childhood*, reports that "there is a robust clinical literature on the child's understanding of death" and that all authors "agree on three periods in the child's emerging understanding of death" (60).[4] Carey summarizes this way the picture that emerges from this developmental literature of the first stage of a child's understanding of death:

In the first period, characteristic of children age 5 and under, the notion of death is assimilated to the notions of sleep and departure. The emotional import of death comes from the child's view of it

as a sorrowful separation and/or as the ultimate act of aggression
. . . In this period death is seen neither as final nor as inevitable.
Just as one wakes from sleep or returns from a trip, so one can
return from death. Although children associate death with closed
eyes and immobility, as in sleep, they do not grasp the totality of
the cessation of function. Nor do they understand the causes of
death. Even though they might mention illness or accidents, it is
clear that they envision no mechanisms by which illness or accidents cause death. (60)

And here is her summary account of the next stage:

The second stage (early elementary years) in the child's understanding of death is transitional and is characterized differently in
the different studies. All authors agree that children now understand the finality of death, and that they understand the sense in
which a dead person no longer exists. However, children still see
death as caused by an external agent . . . The child does not yet
conceptualize death in terms of what happens within the body as
a result of these external events. (61)

And here is the third stage:

In the final stage death is seen as an inevitable biological process.
Such a view of death first becomes evident around age 9 or 10 . . .
To [a] question about the causes of death, one sage 12-year-old
answered, "When the heart stops, blood stops circulating, you stop
breathing, and that's it . . . Well, there's lots of ways it can get
started, but that's what really happens." (64)

No doubt there are various difficulties one might raise with the
claim that these are the stages in which children come to understand what death is. But certainly if this account is even roughly
correct, there is no good reason to try to discuss death, let alone
the death of children as a manifestation of the problem of evil,
with young children, say, children under the age of nine. This is
because younger children will not understand the finality of death.
    One set of ethical issues important in the treatment of almost

all patients, including children, concerns *disclosure.* How much should doctors tell patients about diagnoses and prognoses? The standard developmental account of how children acquire an adequate concept of death suggests that, for stage one or stage two children who are suffering from a life-threatening accident or illness, disclosure is simply a nonissue. Since these patients have only a proto-concept of death and, therefore, only a defective conception of the threat posed by life-threatening accidents and illness, they simply aren't in a cognitive position to have the seriousness of the situation disclosed to them. Perhaps the medical team needs to try to deal with these children's fears in the way one might try to deal with an adult's phobias; but these patients are apparently not cognitively competent to have their true situation revealed to them.

A related issue is *decisionmaking.* What part, if any, should a seriously injured or ill child play in decisions concerning treatment? Even though consent to treatment is not a legal requirement for child patients, perhaps some sort of involvement in the decision process is *morally* required if the child is to be respected as a person in her or his own right. But what sort of involvement?

The relevance of the standard developmental account is, it seems, equally clear here. To play any sort of meaningful role in making decisions concerning one's own treatment, one has to understand something of the seriousness of one's illness or injury and appreciate to an important extent what success and failure in treatment amount to. A child with a limited or defective concept of death is simply not equipped to understand the seriousness of life-threatening illness or injury and, therefore, cannot play any rational role in choosing the best course of treatment.

The standard developmental account of how children come to develop a concept of death thus seems to underwrite a completely paternalistic approach to children under nine years of age with respect both to (1) disclosure of diagnosis and prognosis and (2) consent to treatment. One is encouraged to think that, although

the management of child patients ought to minimize patient distress, it need not, indeed, it *cannot* really, respect patient
autonomy; the cognitive competence required for autonomy is
simply missing in young children.

Before we rest too comfortably in our acceptance of medical
paternalism for child patients, it is worth reflecting on the experience of the children on whom the research on "concepts of
death" was done. The only experience many of them will have
had with death is the death of a pet. Even if a child in the age
range studied has experienced a death in the family, it will much
more likely have been the death of a grandparent than that of a
parent or sibling.

Of course, there are children in this age range who have lost a
parent, sibling, or best friend. And there are children who, themselves, suffer life-threatening accidents or terminal illness. In fact
it was children in this last group that we were focusing on in asking
whether or how much they should be included in the disclosure
of diagnosis or in decisionmaking. But these cases, being excep-
tional, will not have played a significant role in establishing how
children come by a concept of death. We need to ask, specifically,
whether the standard developmental account applies to them.

Here the research of Myra Bluebond-Langner in *The Private
Worlds of Dying Children* is especially relevant. The children Bluebond-Langner studied were victims of acute lymphocytic leukemia. At the time of her study, 1971–72, the prognosis for such
patients was almost hopeless. Fifty patients were included in her
study, thirty-two as "informants," eighteen as "primary informants." Their ages ranged from three to nine. Of the eighteen primary informants, six survived at the end of the nine-month study.
By the time Bluebond-Langner finished writing her book some five
years later, none was still living.

What emerges from Bluebond-Langner's studies is that,
although the children did go through identifiable stages in coming
to understand and deal with the likely onset of their own death,

those stages were correlated with their own life experience with a terminal illness, and not at all with their ages. These are the stages Bluebond-Langner identified:

> The children first learned that "it" (not all the children knew the name of the disease) was a serious illness. [Stage 1] At this time they also accumulated information about the names of the drugs and their side effects. By the time children reached stage 2, they knew which drugs were used when, how, and with what consequences. The third stage was marked by an understanding of the special procedures needed to administer the drugs and additional treatments that might be required as a result of the drugs' side effects . . . But they saw each procedure, each treatment, as a unique event. Not until they reached stage 4 were they able to put treatments, procedures, and symptoms into a larger perspective. By then, the children had an idea of the overall disease process—that the disease was a series of relapses and remissions, and that one could get sick over and over again in the same way, and that the medicines did not always last as long as they were supposed to, if at all. But it was not until the fifth stage that the children learned the cycle ended in death. They realized [then] that there was a finite number of drugs and that when these drugs were no longer effective, death became imminent. (167)

Of course, any child who reached the fifth stage in this process had a conception of death as the irreversible cessation of all biological functions. And any child who reached that stage knew that death would come to her or him, not sometime in the unreal future, but soon. Thus, every leukemic child in Bluebond-Langner's study who reached Stage 5 would have a conception of death that included all the elements in the last-stage concept of the standard developmental account.

Bluebond-Langner's stages might be thought of as Piagetian, except for one crucial feature: the utter irrelevance of the child's chronological age. This feature also puts her account at odds with the standard developmental account.

Bluebond-Langner explains the importance of a child's experience this way:

> The place of experience in the socialization process helps illuminate why a child could remain at a given stage without passing to the next for what seemed an unusual length of time. Tom, for example, remained at stage 4 for a year, whereas Jeffrey remained at stage 4 for only a week. Since passage to stage 5 depended on the news of another child's death, and none had died after Tom reached stage 4, he could not pass to stage 5. When Jennifer died, the first child to die that year, all the children in stage 4, regardless of how long they had been there, passed to stage 5.
>
> The role of experience in developing awareness also explained why age and intellectual ability were not related to the speed or completeness with which the children passed through the stages. Some three- and four-year-olds of average intelligence knew more about their prognosis than some very intelligent nine-year-olds, who were still in their first remission, had had fewer clinic visits, and hence less experience. (169)

Clearly the standard developmental account of how children acquire the concept of death is irrelevant to terminally ill children in a hospital ward with other terminally ill children. One could, perhaps, extrapolate from these findings to conclude that, if we placed children on a continuum from *No direct experience with death at all* at one end to *Terminally ill and in a treatment program with other terminally ill children* at the other, the experience of the vast majority of children would place them somewhere between the two extremes; but perhaps most of them would be closer to the innocence extreme than to the extreme of terminal illness.

The standard developmental account of how children acquire a concept of death is satisfactory, at best, for children in the "normal" range of experience with life-threatening accident and illness, that is, children largely innocent of such experience. It is irrelevant to children with a great deal of such experience. Therefore, it is also irrelevant to ethical issues about whether we should disclose the bleak prognosis to a child with a terminal illness, or enlist the child's participation in treatment decisions.

There is, in fact, some evidence that treating terminally ill children with a real respect for their autonomy by disclosing their prognosis and enlisting their participation in treatment decisions increases dramatically the chances that the children will be healthy of mind and free from severe depression.[5]

No doubt some children who face the real prospect of imminent death also have, for that very reason, important things to tell us and to discuss with us if we are only strong enough to listen and to share. But having a good discussion with such a child, even with the help of a good story like *Tuck Everlasting* or *Charlotte's Web*, requires both an openness to the child and an openness to thinking about death that we adults finds extremely difficult to manage. A terminally injured or ill child is the ultimate threat to our parental pretensions. If we can learn to deal honestly with that threat and to deal respectfully as well as lovingly with such a child, we will have taken a major step in the development of our own maturity.

9

Literature for Children

Is there something inevitably "phony" about stories written by adults for children? Some people have thought so. Jacqueline Rose's book *The Case of Peter Pan* carries the subtitle *The Impossibility of Children's Fiction.*[1] Rose writes: "Children's fiction is impossible, not in the sense that it cannot be written (that would be nonsense), but in that it hangs on an impossibility . . . This is the impossible relation between adult and child" (1).

One thing that Rose thinks makes the relation between adult and child in children's literature impossible is the "rupture" between adult writer and child reader. "Children's fiction sets up the child as an outsider to its own process," she continues, "and then aims, unashamedly, to take the child *in*" (2).

Of course there is an obvious way in which all fiction aims to "take the reader in." Writers of fiction are storytellers who make up stories and tell them as if they were reporting on something that had actually happened.

You may protest that adult readers, at least, are seldom taken in. And by that you would mean that adults typically know they are reading fiction rather than fact, whereas children may be far less clear, both about the general distinction between fact and fiction and also about whether a given story is fact or whether it is fiction.

I'm not at all sure that children, as a general thing, are indeed "taken in" by the stories they read or have read to them. At least I am not convinced that many of them think that what happens in a fictional story "really did happen." Anyway, it isn't taking children in by making them think something purely fictional is factual that most interests Rose. She is more concerned that children's fiction may be motivated by an adult's unhealthy infatuation with an idealized child, an infatuation that may be sexual in some unconscious or repressed way.

I have no wish to play down the motivational complexities to be found in the writers of fiction in general, or writers of fiction for children in particular. Good writers are artists and, as we all know, artists are among the most fascinating subjects for psychological study there are. But I think we should be suspicious of the idea that all, or even most, writers of children's stories have more complex or more questionable motivation than writers of other types of fiction.

For an instructive contrast to Rose's deep suspicions about the writers of children's literature and the stories they write, we might look to a provocative comment from W. H. Auden. "There are good books," Auden wrote, "which are only for adults, because their comprehension presupposes adult experiences, but there are no good books which are only for children."[2] Auden is no doubt right that a good book for children will be one a reader need not have had adult experience to comprehend or appreciate. Auden is also right, I think, in insisting that a good children's book is one a reader need not *lack* adult experience or sophistication to appreciate. And that fact is very important.

If a good book for children is simply a good book that does not presuppose adult experience or sophistication, then there need be no "rupture" in children's literature between writer and audience. How can this be? How can there be books that adults can appreciate fully as much as children? One might suppose that the only way this could happen would be for a book to indulge adult nostalgia for an earlier and more innocent life. If this were right, then a good children's book would have to be phony for another reason. It would have to encourage adult readers to pretend they were children again.

No doubt children's books do often appeal to adult nostalgia. This nostalgia may take various forms. It might be nostalgia for one's own childhood—perhaps nostalgia induced by recollections of hearing this story, or similar stories, as a child. Or it might be nostalgia brought on by thinking about characters or situations in the story that recall one's own childhood. Or the nostalgia might just be a longing for a simpler world, a world as presented to, or through, the eyes of a child.

In the last chapter I discussed two classic children's stories that appeal to adults as well as to children by addressing the existential issue of our common mortality. Natalie Babbitt's *Tuck Everlasting* and E. B. White's *Charlotte's Web* deal with that most frightening issue of all, death, in a genuinely philosophical way, namely, by encouraging us readers, whether old or young, to reflect freshly on the meaning of death. Other children's stories are just as philosophical, even when they are less existential.

Consider the story "The Garden," from Arnold Lobel's wonderful collection *Frog and Toad Together*.[3] In the story Toad, trying to follow the example of his friend Frog, plants seeds in his garden. Finding that the seeds do not immediately sprout and show their sprouts above the soil, Toad shouts at them to grow. Frog tells him he is frightening his seeds. Toad is horrified at the thought that he might have frightened his seeds. To comfort them he burns candles in their vicinity. He sings songs, reads poetry, and plays music to his seeds. When these various efforts produce no observable result, Toad laments, "These must be the most frightened seeds in the whole world." Exhausted, he falls asleep.

Frog wakes Toad up with the joyful news that the seeds have finally sprouted. Toad is, of course, pleased and relieved. He mops his brow and sighs, "But you were right, Frog, it *was* very hard work."

From my own rather extensive experience of reading this story to hearers of all ages, I can testify that it has both an immediate and a lasting appeal. Toad's earnest naiveté inevitably moves us. And we naturally resonate, whether we are four or seventy-four, to the way Frog tries to help his somewhat simple-minded friend. But the real genius of the storyteller shows itself in the last line: "You were right, Frog, it was very hard work." That line gets an appreciative smile and chuckle out of everyone, from age three to eighty-three.

The joke is profound. No reader or hearer really thinks that singing to seeds, playing the violin for their benefit, or reading poetry to them will make them sprout and grow. But why not?

The story, one could say, is a dramatization of a fallacy teachers of informal logic sometimes call by the Latin name *post hoc, ergo propter hoc.* ("After this, therefore because of this.") The mere fact that seed growth follows poetry reading, for example, is not by itself sufficient evidence to establish that poetry reading causes, or even helps cause, seed growth.

Of course, many, many cases of seed growth after poetry reading would be more significant in establishing the causal hypothesis, though perhaps not very much more significant, unless there were also cases like this one except for having *no* poetry reading and then *no* seed growth either. That further finding might suggest the need for yet further investigation. We would want to know if it was really the extra hours of light from burning candles during the all-night vigil that caused seed growth, rather than the poetry reading itself.

And now, of course, we are well launched on the difficult task of trying to say what kind of evidence is necessary and sufficient for establishing that one thing is the cause of another. The general question belongs to philosophy. The specific question about what makes *seeds* grow belongs to botany, or to agriculture, where, in fact, the possible effect of doing something like playing music to sprouts or plants is a matter of genuine controversy.

Toad's earnest remark about it's being hard work to get the seeds to grow is, of course, a joke. But it is the kind of joke that reminds us of our ignorance and uncertainty and encourages us to think more about the matter. In this way it is a philosophically provocative joke. For the adult reader the problem of why the burning of candles is, or is not, a cause of seed growth may lack the freshness and urgency it could have for a child. But vis-à-vis our children we adults have only the pseudo-advantage of knowing what most people conventionally count as real causes rather than false ones. Unless we are rather sophisticated philosophers, we will not be prepared to specify what we consider necessary and sufficient conditions for one event's being the cause of another.

Each of the Lobel stories in this collection includes a line that makes a philosophically provocative joke. Take "Dragons and Giants." That story is about bravery, which, if we are honest, we will also admit we have trouble defining and identifying. The story begins with Frog and Toad asking themselves whether they are brave the way the characters in the story *they* are reading are. *Those* characters fight giants and slay dragons. To determine whether they, too, are brave, Frog and Toad look into a mirror. "We look brave," they report. "Yes, but are we?" they want to know.

To prove they are brave, Frog and Toad set off on a dangerous mission: they climb a mountain. While on their mission they encounter a hawk, a snake, and an avalanche—all natural enemies of frogs and toads. That they survive these threats might count in favor of their bravery, if their activity were not so frenzied and hysterical. In the end they run back to Toad's house, where one jumps into bed and pulls the cover over his head, and the other jumps into the closet and closes the door. They stay in their respective hiding places a very long time, "just feeling very brave together."

The story's final line, "just feeling very brave together," uses genuinely Socratic irony to makes us realize something important.

Confident as we readers are that Frog and Toad in the story are not really brave, we probably can't say what bravery is, at least not in any clearly satisfactory way. Does one have to do something dangerous to be brave? Sometimes, it seems, staying in one's place (even in bed!) rather than running away (perhaps into big sister's bedroom) expresses bravery. Is having a sinking feeling in one's stomach or having one's knees knock and one's teeth chatter even relevant to the question of whether one is brave? We may find it hard to say. But if we can't define 'brave' in any fully satisfactory way, how can we be certain that Frog and Toad are not brave? The joke is not just on Frog and Toad. Whether we are four or forty, the joke is also on us.

Arnold Lobel had a special genius for incorporating Socratic irony into his simplest children's stories. His one-liners have the grace, humor, and profundity of great poetry. Yet *Frog and Toad Together*, because of the utter simplicity of its vocabulary, counts as a primer, an "I can read" book.

For a second example, I choose a story told in an equally economical way, though it is aimed at a somewhat older child. It is *Yellow and Pink* by William Steig.[4] Steig also illustrated his story, and the pictures are an important part of its charm. Still, the story by itself is beautiful.

Two wooden figures, one painted pink, the other yellow, lie on newspapers in the sun, perhaps to dry. They look like marionettes, except for not having strings attached to them. The pink one is short and fat, whereas the yellow one is straight and thin. Each starts to wonder what he is doing there on newspapers in the sun.

When Yellow notices Pink beside him he asks, "Do I know you?"

"I don't think so," Pink replies cautiously.

"Do you happen to know what we're doing here?" Yellow asks. Pink doesn't know.

"Who are we?" asks Yellow.

Pink doesn't know that either.

"Someone must have made us," Pink conjectures.

Yellow produces all sorts of difficulties with Pink's hypothesis and himself proposes, "We're an accident, somehow or other we just happened."

Pink starts laughing. "You mean these arms I can move this way and that," he asks incredulously, "this head I can turn in any direction, this breathing nose, these walking feet, all of this just happened, by some kind of fluke? That's preposterous!"

Yellow is not swayed. He invites his companion to stop and reflect. "With enough time," he says, "a thousand, a million, maybe two and a half million years, lots of unusual things could happen. Why not us?"

With great patience Pink takes up one feature of their construction after another. In each case he challenges Yellow to suggest how that feature could have been the result of an accident. For each feature Pink mentions Yellow tries to say how it could, indeed, have been the result of an accident.

"Suppose," he suggests, "a branch broke off a tree and fell on a sharp rock in just the right way. So there you have legs."

He continues: "Then winter came and this piece of wood froze and the ice split the mouth open. There's your mouth. Then maybe one day a big hurricane took that piece of wood and sent it tumbling down a rocky hill with little bushes, and it got bumped and chipped and brushed and shaped this way and that."

Slowly Yellow imagines accidental events that might have accounted for all features of their construction—arms, fingers, toes, ears, and nostrils. For the origin of eyes he has several suggestions: "Eyes could have been made by insects boring it, or by woodpeckers, maybe even by hailstones of exactly the right size hitting repeatedly in just the right places."

Pink is unimpressed. "How come we can see out of these holes the woodpecker made?" he wants to know.

"Because that's what eyes are for, you dummy," Yellow replies.

When Yellow completes his speculative account of accidental origins, Pink springs on him a further difficulty. "Let's say you're right, just for the sake of conversation," he grants, amiably; "do you mean to tell me all those odd things happened not only once, but twice, so that there's two of us?"

Yellow is unfazed. "Why not?" he throws the question back to Pink: "In a million years, I didn't say five seconds, in a million years the same thing could easily happen twice over." Lest his skeptical friend reject his suggestions too quickly he adds: "A million years takes a long time. Branches do break, winds are always blowing, there's always some lightning, and some hail, and so forth and so on."

Finally a mustachioed man shambles up, examines Pink and Yellow, and announces, with satisfaction, "Nice and dry."

As the mustachioed man takes Pink and Yellow away, tucked under his arm, Yellow whispers in Pink's ear, "Who is this guy?" Pink doesn't know. And so the story ends.

By making his figures wooden, marionette-type dolls, Steig deprives them of the genetic mechanisms of self-reproduction, and so of the possibilities of Darwinian selection across generations. But in that respect his speculative biology is a little like that of the pre-Socratic philosophers Empedocles, Democritus, and Leucippus. They, too, conjectured that accidentally acquired characteristics might turn out to be functional; and they, too, lacked a genetic theory to explain how a chance mutation with adaptive value might be able to pass on its genotype to later generations.

Is it plausible to suppose that all the clearly functional features of living organisms are the result of an incredibly long period of evolutionary selection—from the development of unicellular organisms to the evolution of higher primates, including human beings? Many people assume so, but few of them could give a detailed story of how this might have come about, perhaps not even a story that is significantly more plausible than Yellow's account.

In Steig's story Yellow and Pink fail to recognize their creator. Might it be so with us, too?

William Steig, like Arnold Lobel, uses the format of a story for children to tell a sort of fable. The fable invites the reader, whether child or adult, to reflect on a deeply philosophical and scientific question about how we human beings came to be.

Neither Lobel's *Frog and Toad Together* nor Steig's *Yellow and Pink* is phony. Nor are their authors manipulative. With great poetic simplicity these stories raise questions, including fascinating philosophical questions, that are well worth reflecting on, whether one is a child or an adult.

In restricting my discussion to stories that raise philosophical issues I do not mean to suggest that, within the broad field of children's literature, it is only the philosophical ones that avoid being phony. That is certainly not true. Children's stories can be authentic literature in many, many different ways. But at least one way that a story written by an adult for children can meet the test of authenticity is by raising hard questions with directness and simplicity and also, ideally, with humor!

10

Child Art

When our younger daughter was about four years old she painted
a picture that has become a family favorite. In crimson on a brown
paper background, it depicts, in a simple, pyramidal form, the
heads and shoulders of three human figures. We framed the picture many years ago and have hung it, from time to time, in a
bedroom or family room.

During a house move several years ago I came across the
painting again and stopped to admire its elegance and bright
brashness. Though we haven't yet hung it in our new house, I can
certainly imagine finding a good place for it and thinking that, of
the various options open to us, hanging that particular painting
would be the very best thing we could do with that space.

Of course there are personal reasons why my family and I like
that particular painting. It reminds us of our daughter, whom we
love very much. It recalls an interesting period in her life, and in
our lives. And by now it is familiar to us in a way that makes it
reinforce a sense of continuity in our lives. Suppose, though, that
a friend of ours who is a museum curator were to visit and to view
the painting. (Let's call the painting, which now has no name,
Three Figures in Crimson.) Is it conceivable that a competent art col-
lector might decide that *Three Figures in Crimson* is a significant work
of art, one worthy to be exhibited in, say, the Boston Museum of
Fine Arts?

Of course anyone who tried seriously to answer that question might want more information about *Three Figures*, or about my daughter, and might want to have a look at the painting itself. But would one *need* to have more information, or to look at the painting, to answer the question? Or have I already said enough to make quite clear that the answer is no? To put the question the other way around, could it be a reasonable response for the curator of a major art museum to say that she would have to look at the painting by a young child to determine whether it would be suitable for the museum's permanent collection?

Of course the Boston museum might be doing a special collection to illustrate, so to speak, the natural history of painting and drawing. The curator might want *Three Figures in Crimson* as a fine example of some recognizable style or stage of development in children's painting. I shall explore a little later what it might mean to say that this or that work would make a good addition to a collection of children's art. For the moment, though, let's consider the bigger question. Is it conceivable that *Three Figures in Crimson* might be a good addition to a general collection of art?

In fact, curators don't go around collecting art irrespective of category. They may find something that would make a good addition to their collection of Impressionism, or Flemish art, or Cubism, or Japanese watercolors, or what have you. But they collect work in categories. So even if we don't imagine our friend the curator as mounting an exhibition of children's art, we seem to have to think of her as categorizing *Three Figures in Crimson* in some way or other. Is there a recognized category in which a painting by a four-year-old might excel?

Again, the obvious category for *Three Figures in Crimson* would be children's art. But, again, let's postpone discussing that. Is there some other category into which it might fit?

Recapitulation theories of childhood of the sort we discussed in Chapter 2 suggest that *Three Figures* might be classified as primitive art. But which primitive art? Well, suppose the style were suggestive of some of the prehistoric art of Oceania, say some of the rock or bark art of Western Australia. Perhaps interesting comparisons and contrasts could be made between *Three Figures in Crimson* and certain examples of Australian rock art. Let's suppose the affinities, as well as the points of contrast, were strikingly interesting. Still, that wouldn't mean that my daughter's childhood painting belongs in a museum's collection of Australian rock art. It wouldn't. Nor would it fit into any other recognized category of 'primitive' or tribal art. And the reason is that it isn't primitive or tribal art, no matter what the similarities with such art, and no matter how tempting the idea is that ontogeny recapitulates phylogeny.

If it wouldn't fit into a collection of tribal art, then perhaps it should go into a modern collection. One might note, for example, similarities between *Three Figures in Crimson* and some of the abstractionist paintings Paul Klee did in the 1930s. Maybe it should be added to the museum's collection of abstract art.

It is an important fact about Klee that he was interested in children's art, including, at one point, the drawings and paintings he himself had produced as a child. Indeed, the very first catalogue of his own art begins with examples of art he had produced as a child. And many of his later works, including especially, I should say, many paintings from the last decade of his life, are done in a style suggestive of child art.[1] It is quite conceivable that one of these later works should be strikingly similar to *Three Figures in Crimson*. Does this mean that *Three Figures* might be added, appropriately, to the museum's collection of abstractionism?

Not really. Of course our friend the curator might want to mount a special exhibition of children's art in the company of late Klee. The point might be to help us appreciate the work of Klee done in a childlike style by laying it alongside real children's art. In a similar spirit, one might put examples of African tribal art alongside works by Picasso that were influenced by African art.[2] Again, the point would be to help us to appreciate Picasso by comparing his art with the work that influenced it.

Of course it might work the other way around, too. Picasso

might help us understand tribal art better, and Klee might help us understand child art better. Even so, a special exhibition of Klee and children's art would not tend to show that a child's painting, such as *Three Figures in Crimson*, belongs in the museum's permanent collection of twentieth-century abstractionism, any more than the Picasso-African exhibition would suggest that early African art— or some of it—belongs in, say, the museum's collection of Cubism.

The basic reason *Three Figures* doesn't belong in any of the collections established by mainline art museums is that those collections are defined historically and geographically. Striking as the similarities might be between *Three Figures* and painting or drawing in some categorized period or recognized movement, it wouldn't really belong in a collection of that art because it doesn't belong to that period or movement. Whether art should be collected in some radically different manner is a question I shall not discuss. Suffice it to say that, as art is now collected, *Three Figures in Crimson* wouldn't belong in any collection of any established art museum.

One simple alteration in museum collections would open up the possibility of acquiring *Three Figures in Crimson*. It would be to establish, as an addition, a permanent collection of children's art. I turn now to the question of whether it would be appropriate to establish such a collection and to the broader question of how answering the first question might help us better understand the place of children in our society and culture.

There exist already, of course, museums of childhood. Such places nourish adult nostalgia, but they also serve the more educational purpose of helping us to think about the history, sociology, and anthropology of childhood. Such a museum might reserve a wing for children's art. But the purpose of child art would be to remind us of the phenomenon of children's drawing and painting, to exhibit something of its cultural and historical diversity, and also, perhaps, something of its cross-cultural and historical universality.

In asking whether an *art* museum, indeed a good art museum, should have a permanent collection of children's art we were, however, considering a different interest from any that would be addressed primarily by a museum of childhood. We are asking whether child art might be appropriately celebrated as art, rather than merely regarded as social and cultural artifact. Of course, doing one of those things doesn't necessarily exclude doing the other. The point, though, is that doing one doesn't necessarily *include* doing the other.

More directly relevant to my question would be the phenomenon of museums of child art. In fact there is at least one such institution, the International Museum of Children's Art in Oslo, Norway. Yet, even though this museum has achieved some renown, its success doesn't settle as much as we might first think. Being a museum of child art, it raises in dramatic form, but does not answer, the question about the status and nature of child art. One might think of it as just a specialized art museum in the way that a museum of modern art, of which there are many, or a museum of Impressionist art, is a specialized museum. But one might also think of it as a museum of artistic memorabilia of childhood. In that case, the existence of such a museum would not imply any particular judgment concerning the aesthetic value of the art it contains. In fact, until general art museums of good repute collect child art in the way they collect modern art or Impressionist art, there will be clearly no societal recognition of child art as something worthy of collection for its own aesthetic value.

One might have expected to get some help in answering my question from the persisting efforts of philosophers of art to answer Tolstoy's profoundly simply question 'What is art?' But a little reflection will reveal that such an expectation would be unrealistic. Whether we come to accept the Imitation Theory of what art is, or the Expression Theory, or the Formal, or some other theory, there can be no serious question that some of the drawings and paintings of young children count as art. Indeed, it should count as a criterion of adequacy on any theory of art that it recognize at least some drawings and paintings by children as art. But that does not mean any child art is aesthetically worthy of collection by a major museum.

In a way the question I am asking is a political question. In a society made up completely of children, the children might decide for themselves whether they wanted to celebrate some of the art produced by members of their own "kind." In our society, however, children do not have the power to make such a decision. In our society it would have to be an adult decision—a decision concerning financial resources under adult control—whether to collect children's art for a major museum.

For us, then, the question is whether we adults consider it appropriate or worthwhile to celebrate the aesthetic sensibility and artistic achievement of artistically gifted children. This, in turn, raises political questions about exploitation and about which educational ideals we choose to implement in our society. But it also raises the issue of whether we as adults can recognize anything of profound worth in the work of a child, even a very sensitive and gifted child.

In the aesthetic evaluation of children's art there are certainly enthusiasts as well as detractors. Aldous Huxley must be counted among the most enthusiastic of the enthusiasts. In his introduction to a pamphlet of children's drawings he writes that "when left to themselves," children "display astonishing artistic talents." He goes on:

> How sure is their sense of colour! I remember especially one landscape of a red-roofed house among dark trees and hills that possessed in its infantile way all the power and certainty of a Vlaminck . . . Many of these pastoral landscapes and scenes of war are composed—all unwittingly of course, and by instinct—according to the most severely elegant classical principles. Voids and masses are beautifully balanced about the central axis. Houses, trees, figures

are placed exactly where the rule of the Golden Section demands that they should be placed.[3]

Huxley claims that 50 percent of children are "little geniuses in the field of pictorial art," but that among adults the percentage goes down to one in a million.

The detractors are perhaps even more easily found. I once approached the curator of painting and sculpture at a major art museum (not, I should say, the Boston Museum of Fine Arts) with the suggestion that he mount an exhibition on the theme "Twentieth-Century Art and Children's Art." I suggested he exhibit some well-chosen children's art, both for its own sake and also for the relationship it would bear to the work of Klee, Miró, Dubuffet, and other twentieth-century artists whose work was influenced by child art, or at least seems to show strong affinities with children's art.

This curator agreed that an exhibition along such lines could have great didactic value. Indeed, he even named museums— other than his own—that might be interested in such a show. But he assured me that no children's art would ever be shown in *his* museum as long as he was chief curator. He would allow nothing to be exhibited there, he said, that was not first-rate art; and no children's art, he insisted, was first-rate art.

There is an identifiable position about children and the goods of childhood from which it would follow that this adamant curator was right and Huxley wrong. I suspect that some rather vague version of this position is held by many people in our society, perhaps by most people. It is given a clear statement and a straightforward defense by Michael Slote in his book *Goods and Virtues*.[4]

Slote thinks that the goods of life are relative to the period of one's life. His claim is not just that what can be reasonably pursued as a good for childhood, or for senescence, is different from what can be reasonably pursued as a good for young adulthood, or for middle-age, though he also assumes that to be the case. His claim is the more interesting one that the goods of childhood and the goods of old age are less valuable, indeed much less valuable, than the goods available at the prime of life. To dramatize his point he asks us to weigh the value of good dreams:

> In a way, our treatment of childhood . . . is interestingly similar to the way we regard what happens in dreams. Proust tells us (roughly) that we do not reckon the sufferings and pleasures of our dreams among the actual goods and evils of our lives . . . And just as dreams are discounted except as they affect (the waking portions of) our lives, what happens in childhood principally affects our view of total lives through the effects that childhood success or failure are supposed to have on mature individuals. Thus in cases where an unhappy schoolboy career is followed by (or, as we sometimes like to think, helps to bring about) happy mature years, we think of the later years as compensating for childhood misery, even as wiping the slate clean. (14–15)

In defense of this way of thinking Slote does several things. First, he tries to elicit from his readers the recognition that they share this view with him, even if they have not heretofore given much thought, or even any thought, to the fact that this is indeed their view. Second, he tries to defend the view against the objection that it makes the goals, frustrations, successes, and failures of childhood irrational or perverse much in the way that the goals and frustrations of an addict, under the influence of the addiction, are perverse or irrational. And finally, in response to the objection that this view fails to account for the unity of a human life, he sketches a conception of, so to speak, the contour of human life. The conception is meant to support the idea that prime-of-life goods are much more valuable than those of any other period and even, perhaps, that childhood goods, though they "have value for, or in, childhood," do not have "value *überhaupt*," that is, value "from the perspective of human life as a whole" (17).

It seems to follow from this last point that a child's painting, though it might have great value for, or in, childhood, would probably not have value *überhaupt*. Since child art hardly deserves to be recognized as a distinct curatorial category in major art museums unless some of it has value *überhaupt*, I shall now say a little about the defensibility of Slote's view.

The devaluation of the goods of childhood that Slote both describes and commends to us is embodied, I think, in the very structure of our social institutions. It is adults, after all, and especially adults in the prime of their lives, who determine the reward structure of our institutions and have the greatest influence in applying this structure to the individuals who get exhibitions, listings in *Who's Who*, positions on important boards, and so forth. These structures do allow homage to has-beens in their dotage; but, in general, most prizes go to achievers in the prime of life.

As far as art is concerned, our great museums embody the assessment that the celebration and appreciation of the work of great artists are among life's greater goods. But the treatment of children's art shows that we think of it as having only instrumental and personal value. It has personal value to parents, teachers, and friends associated with the child artist. It has instrumental value insofar as producing it furthers the general development of the child and, in rare cases, the further development of someone who will actually become an important artist. Otherwise, it has no value.

To justify this sort of assignment of values Slote appeals to what is essentially a biological view of the nature and significance of childhood and old age. Here is part of what he says:

> Consider how ordinary people and biologists tend to think of plants and animals over time. Within the life cycle of a given organism a distinction is typically drawn between periods of development and periods of decay, and this distinction is partly marked by treating a certain period of maturity as representing the fullest development of the organism and other periods as leading "up to,"

or "down from," it. In keeping with these distinctions, there is also
a tendency to think of organisms as being most fully what they are
(what they have it in them to be) during maturity, a tendency
perhaps most clearly exemplified in the tradition of making general
reference to organisms by their adult names rather than by names
appropriate to other stages of their life cycle. (We speak of the
parts of a tree's life, not of a seed's or sapling's life, of the development and decline, or old age, of a horse, but not of a colt.) (36)

This biological profile suggests that the stretch of an individual
organism's life that counts as maturity for that organism is also
normative for it. Goods and products from earlier on are devalued
as immature, whereas those that come later are devalued as
belonging to senescence. Applied to the question at hand, the
best reason one could have, it may seem, for refusing to establish
a permanent collection of children's art in a major museum is that
such art would be, perforce, immature art, and therefore inappropriate for collection alongside the most mature artistic achievements of our civilization.

Perhaps there was a time when even the best tribal art of Africa,
Oceania, and North and South America was considered primitive
and therefore, as civilizations go, immature. Not many people, at
least not many prominent people, express that attitude anymore.
Artists in tribal societies are now recognized to have had traditions
and apprenticeships that make it possible to distinguish mature
artists and mature objects of art in a given tribal style. Moreover,
the attitude toward a tribal culture embodied in the supposition
that the whole culture is immature now strikes most of us as both
naive and morally offensive. Tribal art, we now think, is not, as
such, immature.

We cannot, therefore, use the example of tribal art, which is
represented in the collections of some of our most prestigious art
museums, to question the assumption that only mature art deserves
to be collected in major museums. But we can question that
assumption in other ways. We could begin by asking whether
Marcel Duchamp's notorious urinal, *La Fontaine*, or Andy Warhol's

collection of soup cans, is mature art. The notion of maturity doesn't seem to apply here.

Another relevant group of artists to consider are the so-called modern primitives. Is the art of Grandma Moses or Henri Rousseau mature art? The question seems odd. Consider Grandma Moses. Her art is unschooled; it is therefore a form of folk art. It also has about it a childlike naiveté. But, although Grandma Moses painted for the last quarter of a century of her very long life, her work did not move away from that naiveté to anything one could designate, by contrast, as mature art.

The art of a ten- or twelve-year-old child learning to draw in an art class may be said to be immature. Perhaps it is self-consciously directed toward the satisfaction of prescribed norms and principles. Much less clear is whether the art of, say, a four-year-old could be called immature. It is not produced in a self-conscious attempt to satisfy norms or principles. But whether or not it is immature, it certainly does not count as mature art. Maybe it is just non-mature art.

Does the lack of maturity in even the most aesthetically pleasing or exciting work of a four- or five-year-old automatically disqualify it from being collected alongside the best art in our culture and the other cultures we regularly celebrate? If we can assume that modern primitivists like Grandma Moses and Henri Rousseau and conceptual artists like Marcel Duchamp and Andy Warhol do deserve to be collected alongside the best art of our culture, we should conclude, I suspect, that maturity is not a necessary condition for deserving that status.

Suppose lack of maturity fails to *disqualify* children's art from being collected by a major museum. What would qualify it? That is, even if we move away from the biologically based conception of evaluation that Michael Slote relies on and allow that some of the art objects we want exhibited in even our most exalted exhibition halls cannot be called mature, we need a positive reason to select and celebrate in this way the best of children's art.

At this point it may be useful to compare child art with child philosophy. In Chapter 1 I suggested that many young children naturally raise questions, make comments, and even engage in reasoning that professional philosophers can recognize as philosophical. Not only do they do philosophy naturally, they do it with a freshness of perspective and a sensitivity to puzzlement and conceptual mismatch that are hard for adults to achieve. The adult must cultivate the naiveté that is required for doing philosophy well; to the child such naiveté is entirely natural.

I don't mean that children in general, or even some children, are better philosophers than any adults are. That isn't true. Other things besides a willingness to question accepted beliefs and puzzle over problematic concepts are important to doing philosophy well. But there is a freshness, an urgency, and a naturalness about child philosophy that both asks to be celebrated for itself and can help us appreciate the nature and significance of adult philosophy—or better, of philosophy itself. If one focused exclusively on the adult phenomenon, one would have only a truncated conception of what it is that moves people to ask and re-ask those age-old questions.

Might something analogous be true of child art? Might there be in the best children's art something that both asks to be celebrated in and for itself and also can help us appreciate the nature and significance of adult art, indeed, of art in general? I think so. If I am right, then child art needs to be exhibited as much as child philosophy needs to be recognized, and even published.[5]

Attempts to conceive childhood and to evaluate child culture have tended to assume either that children are merely proto-people, to be cherished and nurtured principally for their potential, or else that they are models of innocence and insight to be emulated by adults. Neither assumption is satisfactory.

Children are people, fully worthy of both the moral and the intellectual respect due persons. They should be respected for what they are, as well as for what they can become. Indeed, we can learn from them and let them enrich our lives as, much more obviously, they learn from us and let us enrich their lives. The parent or teacher who is open to the perspectives of children and to their forms of sensibility is blessed with gifts that adult life otherwise lacks.

Yet it is only in certain respects that a child's perspective is valuable to adults. Adults' endeavors can have a rigor, a discipline, and a sense of history that the corresponding children's efforts are bound to lack. Adults' art can have a mastery of technique and a sense of style and of its place in the history of art that is not open to child art. The problem, then, is to learn how to celebrate child art for what it is and can legitimately be, without either condescension or sentimentality.

It is worth noting that both child art and child philosophy should lead us to question Michael Slote's contention that only prime-of-life goods have primary value. Few children grow up to become mature artists and even fewer to become mature philosophers. For many people the art and philosophy of their childhood is never equaled, let alone surpassed, by the art or philosophy of their adult lives. If painting or doing philosophy has any non-instrumental value for them, it is their child art and their child philosophy that have such value.

So, should *Three Figures in Crimson,* or some other work by a four-year-old, be added to the permanent collection of the Boston Museum of Fine Arts? I think so. Will it? That is harder to say. Whether children's art is ever collected by our most famous art museums will depend, I suspect, on whether the currents of modernism further discredit the assumption that maturity is a *sine qua non* for an art object's being worthy of collection by a major art establishment.

If the "maturity assumption" is widely rejected and children's art is collected seriously, that development will, no doubt, have interesting and significant social and political consequences. For one thing, our attitude toward children and toward the value system that systematically devalues their thought, their sensibility, their experience, and the works of their creation will also change. With such change will come changes in the roles we allow to children in our society. I hope I have said enough to suggest that these developments could constitute, not only a step toward children's liberation, but a significant step toward adult liberation as well.

Notes
Acknowledgments
Index

Notes

Introduction

1. See Philippe Ariès, *Centuries of Childhood* (New York: Vintage Books, 1962).

2. Margaret Mead, "An Investigation of the Thought of Primitive Children, With Special Reference to Animism," in *Personalities and Cultures*, ed. Robert C. Hunt (Garden City, N.Y.: Natural History Press, 1967), 213–137.

2. Theories and Models of Childhood

1. *Baby and Child Care*, 3rd ed. (New York: Hawthorn Books, 1968); quotations from 457, 242.

2. G. Stanley Hall, *Adolescence* (New York: D. Appleton, 1904). A splendidly readable history and critique of the recapitulationist theory is to be found in Stephen Jay Gould's *Ontogeny and Phylogeny* (Cambridge: Harvard, 1977).

3. Florence Perry Heide, *The Shrinking of Treehorn* (New York: Dell, 1971). F. Scott Fitzgerald uses a similar idea in his short story "The Strange Tale of Benjamin Button."

4. Anthony Kenny, trans. and ed., *Descartes: Philosophical Letters* (Oxford: Clarendon Press, 1970), 111. John Locke, *An Essay Concerning Human Understanding*, vol. 1, book 2 (New York: Dover, 1959), 121–122.

5. B. F. Skinner, *Science and Human Behavior* (New York: Free Press, 1953), 91.

6. Noam Chomsky, *Knowledge of Language* (New York, Praeger, 1986), xxvi.

7. Some passages in Piaget sound unabashedly recapitulationist. Thus, speaking of his "genetic epistemology," he writes: "the most fruitful, most obvious field of study would be the reconstituting of human history— the history of human thinking in prehistoric man. Unfortunately, we are not very well informed in the psychology of primitive man, but there are children all around us, and it is in studying children that we have the best chance of studying the development of logical knowledge, mathematical knowledge, physical knowledge, and so forth." "Genetic Epistemology," *Columbia Forum* 12 (1969), 4. But Piaget also insists that experience is needed to trigger development (the experientialist model) and that development, for us as well as for our ancestors, proceeds according to "laws" of mental development. Here is an important passage on that last point: "For our part, we do not believe that the possible resemblances between the thought of the child and that of primitive man . . . are due to any kind of heredity. The permanence of the laws of mental development suffice to explain these convergences . . ." "The Mental Development of the Child," in Jean Piaget, *Six Psychological Studies,* ed. David Elkind (New York: Vintage, 1968), 27.

8. Stephen Jay Gould, in *Ontogeny and Phylogeny* (Cambridge, Mass.: Harvard University Press, 1977), esp. 156–161, has a good discussion of the importance of recapitulationism to Freud. He quotes a letter of 1915 to Sandor Ferenczi: "Anxiety hysteria—conversion hysteria—obsessional neurosis—dementia praecox—paranoia—melancholia—mania . . . This series seems to repeat phylogenetically an historical origin. What are now neuroses were once phases in human conditions" (158).

9. In W. Andrew Collins, ed., *Children's Language and Communication,* Minnesota Symposia on Child Psychology, vol. 12 (Hillsdale, N.J.: Erlbaum, 1979).

10. Patricia Kuhl et al., "Linguistic Experience Alters Phonetic Perception in Infants by 6 Months of Age," *Science* 255 (1992), 606–608.

11. John Macnamara, "Cognitive Basis of Language Learning in Infants," *Psychological Review* 79 (1972), 1–13.

12. C. G. Jung, *Psychology and Education* (Princeton: Princeton University Press, 1954), 134.

3. Piaget and Philosophy

1. See especially Piaget's "Children's Philosophies," in *A Handbook of Child Psychology,* 2nd ed., ed. Carl Murchison (Worcester, Mass.: Clark

University Press, 1933), 534–547. "We realize how interesting these explanations [offered by young children] are from the historical point of view. Indeed, they intimately recall the conceptions of Anaximandre, Anaximne, and other pre-Socratics . . . One sees how very readily the law of identification recalls the law of condensation and rarefaction belonging to the pre-Socratic school" (544).

2. Christa Wolf, *Störfall: Nachrichten eines Tages* (Darmstadt: Luchterhand, 1987), 105–106. Hans-Ludwig Freese begins his delightful book *Kinder sind Philosophen* (Berlin: Quadriga Verlag, 1989) with this wonderful passage.

4. Piaget and Conservation

1. London: Routledge and Kegan Paul, 1974. All page references in this chapter are to this book.

2. *De rerum natura* I, 11, 358–368, trans. R. E. Latham, in *The Nature of the Universe* (Harmondsworth: Penguin, 1951), 38.

3. "A Perverse Creation of Science: Anti-Rubber," *New York Times*, April 14, 1987, C8.

5. Moral Development

1. Martin L. Hoffman, "Empathy, Role Taking, Guilt, and Development of Altruistic Motives," in *Moral Development and Behavior*, ed. Thomas Lickona (New York: Holt, Rinehart and Winston, 1976), 129–130.

2. There are complications. Kohlberg and his associates came to speak of heteronomous and autonomous substages for each of the regular stages and also of the possibility of a 'soft' Stage 7. At the same time they seemed to become less confident of Stage 6. See Lawrence Kohlberg, *Essays on Moral Development*, vol. 2: *The Psychology of Moral Development: The Nature and Validity of Moral Stages* (New York: Harper and Row, 1984), chap. 3 and appendix C.

3. Ibid., 640.

4. "From Is to Ought: How to Commit the Naturalistic Fallacy and Get Away with It in the Study of Moral Development," in *Cognitive Development and Epistemology*, ed. Theodore Mischel (New York: Academic Press, 1971), 165.

5. For a time it seemed that there was indeed regression; but refinement of the theory seems to have dealt with the problem. See Kohlberg, *Psychology of Moral Development*, 437–438.

6. J. R. Snarey, "Cross-cultural Universality of Moral Development," *Psychological Bulletin* 82 (1984), 226.

7. Kohlberg, "From Is to Ought," 164.

6. Children's Rights

1. See, for example, the splendidly clear and helpful survey article "Children under the Law," in *The Rights of Children*, Harvard Educational Review Reprint Series, no. 9 (1974), 1–28. A favorite passage from this article for attack by conservative politicians and commentators was this one: "The basic rationale for depriving people of rights in a dependency relationship is that certain individuals are incapable or undeserving of the right to take care of themselves and consequently need social institutions specifically designed to safe-guard their position. It is presumed that under the circumstances society is doing what is best for the individuals. Along with the family, past and present examples of such arrangements include marriage, slavery, and the Indian reservation system" (7). Despite the, no doubt, deliberately provocative character of that last sentence, the stance of the article as a whole is moderate and measured.

2. Lewis Pitts, "Family Values?" *Nation*, September 21, 1992, 268.

3. In the weak version, the Paternalism Principle allows autonomy to be restricted to prevent harm to the agent; in the strong version, it also allows autonomy to be restricted to benefit the agent.

4. *New York Times*, September 26, 1992, A5.

5. *Escape from Childhood* (New York: Dutton, 1974), 18.

6. Howard Cohen, *Equal Rights for Children* (Totowa, N.J.: Littlefield, Adams, 1980), 45.

7. Bob Franklin, "Children's Political Rights," in *The Rights of Children*, ed. Bob Franklin (Oxford: Blackwell, 1986), 24–53. Shulamith Firestone, *The Dialectic of Sex* (New York: Bantam, 1970), 118.

8. Laurence D. Houlgate, *The Child and the State: A Normative Theory of Juvenile Rights* (Baltimore: Johns Hopkins, 1980).

9. Laura Purdy, *In Their Best Interest? The Case Against Equal Rights for Children* (Ithaca, N.Y.: Cornell, 1992), 214–215.

7. Childhood Amnesia

1. *An Essay Concerning Human Understanding*, Book II, ch. 27, sec. 10 (New York: Dover, 1959), 451.
2. What Locke says is actually "same man," using 'man' generically.
3. Locke, *Essay*, Book II, ch. 27, sec. 16, 458.
4. In the Standard Edition of the Complete Psychological Works of Sigmund Freud, vol. 17, ed. James Strachey (London: Hogarth, 1953), 174–175.
5. *Introductory Lectures on Psycho-Analysis*, in the Standard Edition, vol. 15 (London: Hogarth, 1963), 201.
6. Thomas Reid, *Essays on the Intellectual Powers of Man* (1785), ch. 6, "Of Memory."
7. See John Perry's Introduction to *Personal Identity*, ed. John Perry (Berkeley: University of California, 1975), 3–30.
8. Eve Emmanuel Perris, Nancy Angrist Myers, and Rachel Keen Clifton, "Long-Term Memory for a Single Infancy Experience," *Child Development* 61 (1990), 1796–1807.
9. Katherine Nelson, "The Psychological and Social Origins of Auto-biographical Memory," *Psychological Science* 4 (1993), 7–14.

8. Childhood and Death

1. E. B. White, *Charlotte's Web* (New York: Harper Collins, 1980). Natalie Babbitt, *Tuck Everlasting* (New York: Farrar, Straus and Giroux, 1975).
2 Myra Bluebond-Langner, *The Private Worlds of Dying Children* (Princeton, N.J.: Princeton University Press, 1980), 186.
3. L. M. Kopelman and J. C. Moskop, eds., *Children and Health Care: Moral and Social Issues* (Dordrecht: Kluwer, 1989).
4. Susan Carey, *Conceptual Change in Childhood* (Cambridge, Mass.: MIT Press, 1985).
5. R. Nitschke et al., "Therapeutic Choices Made by Patients with End-stage Cancer," *Journal of Pediatrics* 101 (1982), 471–476.

9. Literature for Children

1. Jacqueline Rose, *The Case of Peter Pan* (London: Macmillan, 1984).

2. W. H. Auden, *Forewords and Afterwords* (New York: Random House, 1973), 291.

3. Arnold Lobel, *Frog and Toad Together* (New York: Harper Collins, 1971), 18–29.

4. William Steig, *Yellow and Pink* (New York: Farrar, Straus and Giroux, 1984).

10. Child Art

1. The intriguing and complex story of Klee's relation to child art is very well told in the essay entitled "Klees kindliche Kunst," in O. K. Werckmeister, *Versuche über Paul Klee* (Frankfurt am Mein: Sundikat, 1981), 124–178.

2. As was done in the exhibition " 'Primitivism' in 20th Century Art: Affinity of the Tribal and the Modern" at the Museum of Modern Art in New York, September 1984 to January 1985.

3. Aldous Huxley, *They Still Draw Pictures* (New York: Spanish Child Welfare Association of America, 1939), 3ff. I owe notice of this passage to George Boas, *The Cult of Childhood* (London: Warburg Institute, 1966), 100.

4. Michael Slote, *Goods and Virtues* (Oxford: Clarendon Press, 1983).

5. For a nice consideration of six child artists as artists, rather than as proto-artists, see Sheila Paine, *Six Children Draw* (London: Academic Press, 1981). My own books, *Philosophy and the Young Child* and *Dialogues with Children*, are, among other things, attempts to publish child philosophy.

Acknowledgments

In writing this book I have drawn on articles in the philosophy of childhood I have already published in other forms. Thus Chapter 1 begins with material I published in "What Did the Universe Appear On?" *Journal of Thought* 20, no. 2 (1985), 14–20. Chapter 4 first appeared as "Egocentric Phenomenalism and Conservation in Piaget," *Behaviorism* 17 (1989), 119–128. Chapter 5 first appeared as "Concept Formation and Moral Development" in *Philosophical Perspectives on Developmental Psychology*, ed. James Russell (Oxford: Blackwell, 1987), 175–190. Chapter 10 appeared as "Child Art and the Place of Children in Society" in *Children, Parents and Politics*, ed. Geoffrey Scarre (Cambridge: Cambridge University Press, 1989), 157–167. Chapter 3 is scheduled to be published in *Philosophy, Democracy and Children*, ed. John P. Portelli and Ron Reed (Calgary: Detselig Enterprises, forthcoming). I wish to thank the respective editors and publishers for permission to use those articles and chapters in this book.

Index

136

Index